PRESSURE?
NO PROBLEM!

A Practical Guide for Dealing
with the Stress in Our Lives

MICHELLE STEELE

ACW Press
Ozark, AL 36360

Pressure? No Problem!
Copyright ©2004 Michelle Steele

Cover Design by Alpha Advertising
Interior Design by Pine Hill Graphics

Packaged by ACW Press
1200 Hwy 231 South #273
Ozark, AL 36360
www.acwpress.com
The views expressed or implied in this work do not necessarily reflect those of ACW Press. Ultimate design, content, and editorial accuracy of this work is the responsibility of the author(s).

Library of Congress Cataloging-in-Publication Data
(Provided by Cassidy Cataloguing Services, Inc.)

Steele, Michelle.
    Pressure? No problem! : a practical guide for dealing with the stress
    in our lives / Michelle Steele. -- 1st ed. -- Ozark, AL : ACW Press,
    2004.

        p. ; cm.
        ISBN: 1-932124-41-1
        1. Stress management. 2. Stress management--Religious
    aspects. 3. Stress (Psychology)--Religious aspects. 4. Time
    pressure--Religious aspects. 5. Spiritual life. I. Title.
BF575.S75 S74 2004
155.9/042--dc22   0409

Printed in the United States of America.

Dedication

I dedicate this book to my wonderful husband. You are my dream partner, my faith builder, and my best friend. Thank you for teaching me, pushing me, believing in me, and stretching me beyond my comfort zone. In you, I witness the steadfastness of God's love. In you, I find the faithfulness of a love I've always dreamed of. I am honored to invest my life with you.

Contents

Foreword

We live in a time of increased activity, anxiety, and pressures. As tension mounts, God's supply of peace, power, and victory comes pouring into the Body of Christ through faithful servants like Michelle Steele. Pressure? No Problem! is a God-given message to bring that victory into your life.

Pastor Paula White
Without Walls International Church

Preface

My prayer is that as you read this book you reach beyond your circumstances and fasten your faith around a determined decision to overcome the pressures of your life. I want you to win. I want you to receive what you are reaching for. For those of you who have become so weary that you have ceased to reach, I want to build within you a courage to reach again.

There are possibilities within your grasp. There is potential within arms' reach. While pressures have mounted against your progress, against your possibilities, and against your potential, Jesus has provided you with victory. May *Pressure? No Problem!* well up in your inner man and be proclaimed from your lips as you break free to progress.

Pressure? No Problem! 1

Pressure. Pressure on the job. Pressure in the marriage. Pressure in the finances. Every person on this earth has some form of pressure to deal with in his or her life. Pressure is the devious force responsible for many failed marriages, nervous breakdowns, and even suicides. Pressure is not age discriminatory; it targets the young and old alike. Pressure attacks regardless of race, nationality, or religious belief.

Pressure has come to steal your peace, paralyze your faith, and keep you from your goal. Believer, listen up! We are designed to float in the flood, be refined in the fire, and soar in the storm. What should the believer say about pressure? "Pressure? No problem!"

The Word of God instructs us to "be vigilant and cautious at all times" (I Peter 5:8 AMP) because our enemy is looking for "someone to seize upon and devour." Second Corinthians 2:11 says, "We are not ignorant of his devices". The Amplified translation says, "We are not ignorant of his wiles and intentions." Just as the roar of a lion is intended to paralyze its prey, pressure is the devil's roar. It is intended to paralyze our faith and leave us vulnerable to his attack. The lion's prey has yet to feel the hot breath of the lion on his neck or the sharp puncture of the fangs through his skin, yet the roar has attacked his senses and his senses responded to that sound. Pressure need only threaten to destroy and many people cower and respond to that threat.

Let's look at a practical example. In Matthew 14, we read the account of Jesus walking on the water. His disciples cry out in fear, thinking He is a ghost. Jesus speaks, commanding good cheer to take the place of their fear. Peter says, "Lord, if it be thou, bid me come unto thee on the water" (vs. 28). Jesus responds to his request with one word: "Come." Peter steps out of the boat and onto that word. Here we witness Peter doing a miraculous thing. Peter is walking on the water, sustained by that one word, "Come." What a victory!

But in the midst of that victory, pressure comes. Verse 30 explains that Peter saw the wind was boisterous. The pressure of seeing that wind paralyzed his faith, and Peter began to sink. The Amplified Bible says, "When he perceived and felt the strong wind" (Matthew 14:30). Pressure is designed to pervert your perception because your perception affects your believing. Peter perceived the strong wind after he was already walking on the water; his perception wasn't focused on the wind until that moment. Peter was focused on the word. Peter was focused on Jesus. After he steps out on the word, pressure distorts his focus, and his faith is paralyzed.

The wind was not a determining factor to Peter's walking on the water. The wind was blowing long before Peter stepped out on the water. Verse 24 tells us that their boat was beaten by the waves and the wind was against them. Peter walked on the water despite the wind. The wind didn't stop him. The Bible does not say that the wind blew him over or that Peter couldn't stand against the force of the wind. The wind was not the factor that caused Peter's failure. Peter's response to the pressure of the situation was the defeating factor. The pressure you are facing today is only a threat. Don't give up just because the wind is blowing. Don't quit believing because of what you see, hear, or feel. Belief will overpower the pressure—as long as you don't give in to what the pressure wants you to see.

Peter, being a fisherman acquainted with storms and the effect of winds on a sea vessel, allowed his senses, knowledge, and previous experience to overrule the Word in his life. People are trained to react to situations based on previous experiences and what our senses reveal. But as believers, we have to renew our minds to perceive every situation through the Word. Peter needed to cast down that thought and remain focused on that one word capable of sustaining him: "Come."

Jesus reprimanded Peter sternly. "Why did you doubt?" Jesus never tolerated doubt. Peter didn't have to be overcome by pressure, and Jesus was upset that Peter succumbed to the circumstance. Do you think Jesus has changed His attitude? Jesus knows the power of the Word and the ability He has placed within us to overcome pressure. Surely, He expects as much, if not more, out of the New Testament believer. (Selah—pause and think on that)

Finally, verse 32 declares, "When they got into the boat, the wind ceased." When the pressure accomplished its mission, it was no longer an issue. Have you ever been fighting, believing, and standing for something but given up because of the pressure of worry, fear, or doubt? Later, when looking at the situation from a clear perspective, you wondered why you gave up so easily. Peter may have felt that same frustration as he looked around at clear skies remembering the feel of the water under his feet.

2 Face the Challenge

The story of David, a young shepherd, is another account that exemplifies how the response to pressure determines victory or defeat. David was anointed in I Samuel 16:13, and the Spirit of the Lord came upon him. From that moment, David reacts to pressure in an extraordinary way. As David steps onto the battlefield, he witnesses professional soldiers running in fear at the sight of Goliath, trembling at the sound of his voice. David's reaction was vastly differently than that of the soldiers. David was incensed at the nerve of this loud-mouthed, oversized, noncovenant fool who was bashing his God.

Goliath was spewing threats and obnoxious warnings of what he was going to do. Goliath hadn't struck any blows. He hadn't killed anyone. He only threatened. The soldiers, who should have been prepared for this kind of pressure, were frightened by what their senses told them: "This guy is big!"

Saul, the king, was the one most qualified in size to face this challenge. In I Samuel 9:2, we find that Saul was head and shoulders taller than anyone in the country. Yet, we find Saul hiding in his tent, overwhelmed by the pressure.

David perceived the pressure through the eyes of his relationship to his God. David knew that God was with him. This challenge was no match for his God. When we know our covenant and the stability of our relationship with our Father, challenges will appear small in comparison.

David declares his attitude toward pressure by saying, "I stood against the lion and the bear when they threatened to destroy me. I defeated the lion. I defeated the bear. Pressure?

No problem! Goliath is just another challenge waiting to be overcome."

Step up to the plate with an attitude of victory and declare to the enemy, "Whatever you throw, I will knock it out of the park!" The challenge you are facing today is just a stepping-stone to your destiny. It was the defeat of the challenge (Goliath) that propelled David into God's plan for his life.

Stop accepting your obstacle as your stopping point. The enemy places the pressure of that obstacle in your path to stop your advancement. The devil doesn't want you to reach God's destination for your life. He throws up the challenge expecting you to back down. He has had plenty of practice with his pressure tactics. But God has an even better track record of triumphing over them.

From God's perspective, you have the ability to conquer this challenge. God will not allow us to be tempted (challenged) above what we are able to bear. With every challenge, God provides a way to escape. First Corinthians 10:13 says, "But God is faithful [to His Word and to His compassionate nature] and He [can be trusted] not to let you be tempted and tried and assayed beyond your ability and strength of resistance and power to endure, but with the temptation He will [always] also provide the way out [the means of escape to a landing place], that you may be capable and strong and powerful to bear up under it patiently" (AMP).

I like to explain God's involvement in our challenges this way. A professional fighter has a professional trainer who prepares him for the fight. The trainer knows the day of the fight, the size and the strength of the opponent, and what it will take to defeat the challenger. The trainer will work with the fighter every day to make sure he is prepared to face this challenge. The trainer would never agree to put his lightweight fighter in the ring with a heavyweight champion. Most of the time, he will start with a challenge he knows that his fighter can conquer. This builds his fighter's confidence and provides experience in dealing with pressure.

God is our trainer. He knows every tactic the enemy has up his sleeve. If we will listen to His instructions, God will prepare us for every challenge long before it comes. God knows that we can win. He would not allow us to face a challenge that we were not capable of defeating.

The trainer sets a schedule of exercise and nutrition that the fighter must follow. The trainer will push the fighter beyond what the fighter thinks he can do. In the same way, God may be dealing with you about prayer and study. God may be leading you to fast and to prepare yourself spiritually. Listen to His instructions. He is preparing you to face the challenge.

David faced the pressure of his challenge by declaring the end at the beginning. He boldly stated that he would do to the giant the same thing he had done to the bear and the lion. David declared what he would do, and then he declared what God would do. "I will overcome this pressure in my life! God will give me victory in this situation!"

David steps out on the battlefield and, lo and behold, pressure starts talking to David. That giant mocked David because of his age, size, and weaponry. Isn't that what your pressure says to you? "You can't stand against me. You don't have enough faith to get healed. You are too far in debt. You are going under. What are you going to do with the Word, quote it against me?"

David outtalked his pressure, and you can, too. Just put God's Word in your mouth in the face of your adversary. "I am the head and not the tail. I am above and not beneath. I am always going over and never going under. Thanks be unto God who always causes me to triumph in Christ Jesus. I am more than a conqueror. I am an overcomer by the blood of the Lamb and the word of my testimony. I have the victory that overcomes the world—MY FAITH!" That will slap pressure in the mouth!

God was preparing David to rule and reign, one challenge at a time. Each challenge prepared him for the next obstacle. Each victory makes your faith muscles stronger. When I was first born again, I knew nothing about God or His kingdom principles. I began believing God for gas money to get to church and grocery money to feed my family. My husband and I began to tithe, exercising our faith for the money to pay our bills. Each bill was a challenge in itself. We faced that lack and began to resist it by speaking the Word. Our situation was drastic and we took drastic measures to combat it. My Scripture list continued to grow until it took an hour each day to confess them all. On three separate occasions, my husband sowed his entire check into God's kingdom. We needed radical seed for a radical harvest. As we overcame each financial challenge, our faith continued to grow. God brought us out of lack and into abundance! Glory to God!

The same faith that we practiced to believe God for gas money is now used for even larger challenges. In the church we pastor, we have a program called "The Back to School Blast" that supplies backpacks and school supplies to needy children. That faith we exercised in our finances is now used to trust God to supply the five thousand backpacks and school supplies that we distribute to our community.

Face the challenge in your life with a new state of mind—the victory state of mind. God is for you. God is with you. That means that pressure is no problem!

3 Pressure Perverts Perception

L et's investigate a statement made in the first chapter. Pressure comes to pervert your perception of the situation. Pervert means to cause to turn or deviate from what is right or normal. In the case of Peter's water walking experience, we see pressure turning the focus of his perception from the word "come" to the presence of the wind and waves.

Proper perception is very important to the success and progress of the believer. Perception is the awareness of your surroundings and circumstances through your physical senses and how your mind interprets the information collected by your senses. Having been translated from the kingdom of darkness into the Kingdom of Light, we must develop our senses to operate in God's kingdom to produce proper perception. If a person had lived all of his life in a jungle and was suddenly introduced to life in the United States, that person would have to develop an understanding of his new environment. Without proper guidance and instruction, that person would have difficulty knowing how to use running water, refrigeration, VCRs, and cell phones. We have many people who have changed kingdoms but have not been taught how to renew their mind, change their will, and control their emotions. They have new resources and abilities available to them in the Word of God, the name of Jesus, and His blood, yet they are unaware how to implement these assets in their lives.

Perception in born-again people differs from unbelievers in that we are not limited to our physical senses. We have spiritual senses through our relationship with God. Yet, the mind still collects and filters the information that enters the heart. How your mind interprets information is very important. Paul prays for the church at Ephesus, that the eyes of their understanding would be enlightened, that they would know the hope of His calling, and that they would be able to comprehend and know the love of Christ (Ephesians 1:18; 3;19). Never again believe the lie that "what you don't know won't hurt you." What you don't know can kill you!

> *And be not conformed to this world: but be ye transformed by the renewing of your mind, that ye may prove what is that good, and acceptable, and perfect, will of God.* Romans 12:2

> *Don't act like people of this world. Instead, be changed inside by letting your mind be made new again. Then you can determine what is good, pleasing, and perfect—what God wants.* Romans 12:2 SEB

The natural mind cannot accurately perceive godly love or a godly life without being renewed in perception. After accepting Jesus as my Lord, I had two major questions: "What is the will of God for my life?" and "How do I hear from God?" I had not been raised in church and knew nothing about God. (I thought these church people were nuts, hearing from God all of the time.) I found the answer to both of those questions as I began to put God's thoughts in my mind. I began to understand the ways of God, the principles He operates, and the desires He had for my life. The will of God has unfolded before me as I have renewed my thinking.

Look at it this way. Your mind is like a computer. Over the years, all your memories, experiences, and thoughts have been programming your computer. When we come to God and are born again, our mind is full of "stinking thinking." There is no magical delete button on your brain. You have to take the time and effort to reprogram your mental hard drive. Line upon line and precept upon precept, we begin to cancel out the old way of thinking and develop proper perception that lines up with what God thinks.

Can two walk together, except they be agreed? Amos 3:3

For us to walk where God is leading and enter into His plan of progress, we must think in line with God. You might as well give up trying to make God see things your way. He is not going to start thinking like you. You are the one who will start thinking like Him. Start taking those thoughts of pressure and perceiving them through thoughts of faith.

Let's define pressure in light of what we now know about perception. Pressure is defined as the application of continuous force, a constraining influence upon the mind or will, a burdensome, distressing, oppressive, or weighty condition. This force and influence upon our minds is intended to turn our awareness of the situation from what God says to what doubt says.

The pressure of the doctor's report weighs on your mind against the perception of "by His stripes ye were healed" (I Peter 2:24). The pressure of the symptom applies force to your mind and causes doubt as to whether or not God has healed you. The pressure of debt and lack distresses you and burdens your thoughts: "What if I don't have gas money to go to church?" or "What if my utilities get turned off?" God's perception is that we have abundance and no lack. Recognize and resist the pressure!

Let's consult II Corinthians 10:3-5 for our weaponry to resist pressure. We find in verse five that the weapons of our warfare are successful in "casting down imaginations and every high thing that exalts itself against the knowledge of God and bringing into captivity every thought to the obedience of Christ." Notice that all of this takes place in your mind—the place of perception.

Casting Down Imaginations 4

The imagination is an engine that transforms thoughts into ambitions, desires, goals, and actions. Just like a gasoline engine turns fuel into energy, the imagination provides a combustion chamber for information and thoughts. God designed our imagination for our success, not our defeat.

Joshua 1:8 is God's strategy for success: "This book of the law shall not depart out of thy mouth; but thou shalt meditate therein day and night, that thou mayest observe to do according to all that is written therein: for then thou shalt make thy way prosperous, and then thou shalt have good success." God is instructing Joshua to monitor and select the information that will be processed through his imagination. The "book of the law," God's Word, was to be the fuel for his meditation and imagination. This is God's guarantee for a successful life.

We confirm this instruction by Psalm 1:1-3: "Blessed is the man that walketh not in the counsel of the ungodly, nor standeth in the way of sinners, nor sitteth in the seat of the scornful. But his delight is in the law of the Lord; and in his law doth he meditate day and night. And he shall be like a tree planted by the rivers of water, that bringeth forth his fruit in his season; his leaf also shall not wither; and whatsoever he doeth shall prosper." To meditate is to concentrate on one thing or to contemplate. God means for us to concentrate on what He said about our situation. The Bible says "day and night." When it is day, imagine what God said in Psalm 1 taking place in your life. When it is night, think on what God said about your life. We must constantly make room for the Word in our thoughts, or pressure will make room for worry, fear, and anxiety in our imaginations.

Have you ever found yourself thinking about a certain bill? The more you think about how much that bill needs to be paid and what might happen if it doesn't get paid the more agitated you become. Before you realize it, you are snapping at your spouse and walking around with a frown. But nothing has actually changed! You have imagined what might happen, and you are acting like it already happened.

Before I gained control of my thoughts, I was a champion worrier. Worry was a practiced thought pattern, like a reflex. It was comfortable to me. A thought would begin like this, *I wonder when my husband will get home.... That seems like a harmless enough thought.* But, watch the process of pressure: *The roads are slippery because of the rain. His tires are worn; what if he gets tire trouble? Maybe that is him now.* I would go look out the window, up and down the street. *Well, he should be home any minute. I wonder if he took enough gas money. I sure hope he doesn't run out of gas. Maybe I should call his work and find out how long ago he left. What if he has had a wreck? Oh, my! He could be hurt. He's always home by now. He would have called me if he were going to be late. I just know that something has happened to him.* By this time, I have planted myself by the window, steaming up the windowpanes with my nose pressed against the glass, straining to see the end of the road. My stomach has developed a nervous flutter, and my heart is beating rapidly in my chest. Why? I let my imagination run wild. My emotions, actions, and physical body had responded to my imagination.

Perhaps you will recognize this scenario. You walk into the church and see Sister So-and-So. She looks at you with a funny look on her face and turns to the woman standing next to her, begins talking, and they both laugh. The thought that comes to your mind is, *They are talking about me.* As the evening goes on, your imagination begins to elaborate as you think, *Is it my dress? Why would she be talking about me? I haven't done anything to her. Who does she think she is? I could say a few things about her, too.*

When the service ends, and Sister So-and-So comes to say hello, you are fit to be tied. But Sister So-and-So had just happened to look your way in the middle of her conversation and hadn't even seen you walk in. Your imagination has affected your anger and your actions.

I found a scripture that helped me gain control of my imaginations. First Peter 1:13 tells us to "Gird up the loins of our mind." This brings to my mind an image of a girdle. We need to place a restraint on our minds because we are letting it all hang out. Quit allowing your imagination to run wild with you. Take control of your thoughts!

The phrase "gird up the loins" actually means to prepare for strenuous effort. Prepare your mind for the pressure of the situation. The Amplified Bible says to "brace up" your mind. A brace is a frame that holds in place or fortifies. The Word will frame up and fortify your mind against the worry, fear, and anxiety that is applying continuous force against your mind.

5 Cast Down Every High Thing that Exalts Itself

Remember, our text is still explaining what the weapons of our warfare are capable of. God has equipped you and I with the ability to cast down the information that tries to exalt itself against God's knowledge in our life.

Second Corinthians 2:11 declares that we are not ignorant (lacking knowledge) of Satan's devices. The word "devices" is from the Greek word noema, which is defined as "perceptions, purpose, the intellect, mind, thought." We should be prepared for the perceptions and thoughts that the enemy is trying to trick us into thinking. His trick is to put us in the wrong frame of mind and have us thinking wrong thoughts. He knows that how you think affects how you believe.

From the beginning, the devil has employed the same tactics in his attempts to separate man from God's plan. In Genesis 3, we see the first example of Satan's devices at work. Satan didn't shackle and tie Eve's hands behind her back to get her to eat the fruit of the tree of the knowledge of good and evil. Satan didn't threaten to kill Eve or her husband if she didn't eat the fruit. Satan applied pressure to her thinking.

"Hath God said?" was the first pressure attack. In order for the devil to exalt earthly knowledge above God's knowledge, he must cause you to question what God said and what God really meant. Believers must establish their belief system on the integrity of God's Word. God meant what He said and said what He meant! We must know that when God said, "I am the Lord that healeth thee" (Exodus 15:26), He meant exactly what He said. We must be assured that when God said, "I am the Lord thy

God that teaches you to profit" (Isaiah 48:17), He meant exactly what He said. Instead, Christians have allowed other thoughts to override God's thoughts. "Well, God put this sickness on me so I could go the hospital and witness to the nurse." "God has kept me poor so that He could keep me humble." This mindset is totally against the mind of God, but people who love the Lord will accept these thoughts.

Eve had a problem. Eve wasn't established on God's Word. In Genesis 3:2-3 we see the flaw in Eve's foundation: "And the woman said unto the serpent, We may eat of the fruit of the trees of the garden: But of the fruit of the tree which is in the midst of the garden, God hath said, Ye shall not eat of it, neither shall ye touch it, lest ye die." God had not said that the tree could not be touched. As a matter of fact, God had given man the responsibility to dress and to keep the garden.

Because Eve was not established on God's Word, she became easy prey for the next attack of pressure—the lie. "Ye shall not surely die." To exalt his knowledge above God's knowledge, Satan gets us to exchange God's truth for his lie. If Eve had built her faith on what God had said, she would have laughed at Satan's lie. She would have never played into his hands. Instead, Eve became a pawn in Satan's devious plan by giving credence to the lie.

Without missing a beat, the enemy's voice continues to administer pressure on Eve's thoughts as he twists Eve's mind against the goodness of her Father. "For God doth know that in the day ye eat thereof, then your eyes shall be opened, and ye shall be as gods, knowing good and evil" (Genesis 3:5). This subtle remark insinuates that God was trying to keep something good from them. In actuality, God's command was protection to them.

Why do so many people perceive the Ten Commandments as the Ten Restrictions? Understand that God is the ultimate parent. He protects us through His instructions. When I tell my six year old that she cannot play on the highway, it is for her own protection. I am not trying to keep her from enjoying life and experiencing life to the fullest. I am protecting her so that she can live and enjoy her life. God understood that there was evil attached to that tree. His intent was to protect His children from knowing, through experience, that evil.

My children don't have to partake of cocaine to know it is not right for them to do. I have told them it is wrong. I have told them it would hurt them if they partook of it. If they will listen to my voice, they will never have to experience that evil for themselves. That is the attitude God wanted Eve to display. God specifically said, " You will die if you eat of that tree."

Nevertheless, Eve was not basing her choices on God's Word. Pressure had perverted her perception. Satan had exalted his knowledge above the knowledge of God in her thinking, and Eve took the fruit, ate it, and gave it to her husband with her. Adam ate it, and the rest is history. Pressure robbed Adam and Eve of God's best for them.

Wait a minute. What about Adam? The Bible tells us that Adam was not deceived (I Timothy 2:14), yet he had pressure of his own that he failed to deal with. God specifically rebukes Adam for listening to the voice of his wife (Genesis 3:17). God gave Eve influence as a helpmeet to Adam. The enemy used her position of influence to pressure Adam into a decision that ruined his life.

Let me take this opportunity to admonish the ladies for a moment. You are the one closest to your husband's heart and closest to his ear. God has given your husband authority in your home. He also has equipped you with influence. It is an asset— your resource. Use it wisely! Proverbs 14:1 says that a wise woman builds her house and a foolish woman plucks it down with her hands. Don't be foolish when it comes to your influence. God's purpose is for your influence to guide your man closer to God's plan. Your influence should encourage him when he is feeling low, strengthen him in the middle of the battle, protect him when he is being tempted, and celebrate him when he does the right thing.

What happens in many marriages is that we take our influence too far. That turns into manipulation. When our man doesn't act the way we want, we begin to nag, nag, nag! Why doesn't the Bible warn us women about a nagging husband? Because, nagging is influence gone bad. We apply pressure to our husbands with complaining, murmuring talk. God said it is better to live on the roof with no protection from the weather than to have to put up with a brawling woman (see Proverbs 21:9 AMP). The wife who abuses her influence is being used as a pressure weapon against her husband and her home. The sad thing is that most women don't recognize what has happened until it is over.

Let me soften the blow a little bit by appealing to your empathy. I confess there was a time in my marriage where I fit the description of the "brawling woman." I was a true nag! When my husband didn't give me my way, I made him pay. I had an arsenal of weaponry to use against him: the silent treatment, the ice cube in the bed, the pitiful pout. I was manipulating my God-given authority. I found out that God couldn't bless my mess; I had to change my mind and my attitude.

In order for God to use us as the husband and wife team that we are today, I had to be willing to lay aside my fleshly fits and be obedient to God. Today, God can use me to influence my husband in business decisions and plans for the future. My husband can trust my voice to agree with God's voice because he has seen and recognized my dedication to God's Word. That trust took time to develop. I won't waste that influence on fleshly opinions. There are very crucial decisions in our lives that could be ruined if I influence him with emotions or information based on my senses. I've got to guard my influence and protect my home.

6 Bringing into Captivity Every Thought

The final purpose of our God-given weaponry is to arrest or take captive thoughts that are sent to destroy us. Too many of us have not exercised authority over our thought life. Thoughts of fear, anger, worry, or depression come, and we entertain them. We open up the door, invite them in and make them comfortable. Inadvertently, we introduce thoughts into our minds that lead to more destructive thoughts; we become desensitized to deadly thought patterns.

Allow me to share an example from my own life. For forty days, my family fasted television as a sacrifice to God. The television was not turned on at all during that time. At the end of forty days, we gradually went back to television being a part of entertainment in our home, and I was shocked by what had happened. During the time that we had fasted, pharmaceutical companies had come out with various drug commercials. They usually start with a list of symptoms they want you to check to see if you have. Immediately, the natural reflex is to take mental inventory, Do I have that symptom? This leads to other thoughts, I do have this symptom and that symptom. Watch it now! God said, "By His stripes, you are healed." Don't meditate on symptoms. You are going to find what you are looking for.

Most of the people I asked didn't seem shocked by these commercials. They had seen so many that it didn't even register to them what was happening. We should be cautious of insensitivity to an idea. You have to be sensitive to every thought that is being introduced into your thinking. Does it agree with what God thinks?

To demonstrate the ability of taking thoughts captive, Jesus placed Himself in the position of temptation. Satan doesn't attack with a pitchfork and pointy ears. Satan doesn't put his hands on Jesus to force Him or frighten Him into doing anything. Satan attacks with pressure: "If thou be the Son of God." Jesus didn't let those thoughts have any ground in His mind. He opened His mouth and let His sword fly, "It is written…." Each thought that the devil threw His way, Jesus nullified it by speaking God's Word.

During the Persian Gulf War, the enemy would aim a Scud missile toward the U.S. armed forces, and the U.S. forces would immediately send a Patriot missile to blow up the Scud in midair. That is how the Word of God destroys the enemy's thoughts. But, we have to speak God's Word in order for it to be launched.

Notice that Jesus didn't ignore the attacks from Satan. Jesus didn't say His opinion or tell the devil, "Don't you know who I am?" Jesus opened His mouth and said what God said. He didn't let the devil even get comfortable talking to Him. Eve should have made the devil a little more uncomfortable by quoting what God said. If you want to make sure Satan stays uncomfortable around you, surround yourself with an atmosphere of God's Word. Talk God's kind of talk. Say what God says. Your enemy can't stand the pressure of God's Word.

How we perceive our stand in the situation is determined by what thoughts we have accepted and allowed to remain in our thinking. There are many thoughts that you should not accept or even allow into your mind. Jesus said in Matthew 6,

Therefore take no thought, saying, What shall we eat? or,
What shall we drink? or, Wherewithal shall we be clothed?
Matthew 6:31

When a thought of failure or fear comes into your mind, don't speak that thought. If you do, you take ownership of it. Refuse that thought, by saying, "That is not my thought." Jesus was explaining in Matthew 6 that worry accomplishes nothing for your good. Worry can't increase you, heal you, or comfort you. As a matter of fact, worry is scientifically proven to make you sick.

> *Finally, brethren, whatsoever things are true, whatsoever things are honest, whatsoever things are just, whatsoever things are pure, whatsoever things are lovely, whatsoever things are of good report; if there be any virtue, and if there be any praise, think on these things.* Philippians 4:8

You have a choice in what thoughts you think. Choose to think on these things instead of everything the circumstance has to say. Being selective in your thought processes is vital to your victory. God has given us a sound mind—the mind of Christ. We are instructed to

> *Let this mind be in you, which was also in Christ Jesus.* Philippians 2:5

God won't force you to have the mind of the anointing, but He has given you access to it. A sound mind is governed by the Word of God.

The Attitude of Non-Resistance   7

In order to have a successful strategy in overcoming pressure, we must first examine the attitude you have toward the situations in your life. There is a myth that has been accepted in the Body of Christ that will mislead you into an attitude of nonresistance. This myth leads people to believe that once they give their lives to Jesus, trouble, situations, and circumstances will never again occur in their lives. "Now that I am saved, I will never have to face pressure or trials again." Then, trouble comes knocking, pressure begins to mount, and those people blame God. "God, how could you let this happen?" "What have I done wrong?" Other people in the church look down at these brothers and sisters who need their prayer support because, after all, they must be sinning for that trouble to be attacking their life. From what chapter and verse did we get that idea?

This misconception produces feelings of failure and condemnation when problems and pressure arise. "Am I really saved?" "Do I have sin in my life because I'm broke or sick?"

God never said that trouble, pressures, or trials would never come against our lives. In actuality, Jesus warns us in John 16:33 that it will:

These things I have spoken unto you, that in me ye might have peace. In the world ye shall have tribulation: but be of good cheer; I have overcome the world.

The word "tribulation" is actually defined "pressure" in the Greek language. You will have pressure, but you don't have to be under pressure. The Amplified Bible says,

Be of good cheer [take courage, be confident, certain, undaunted]! For I have overcome the world. [I have deprived it of power to harm you and have conquered it for you..

Peace is our force to press against pressure.

God expects His presence to give us an attitude of peace. The Lord admonishes in Isaiah 43: 1b-2,

Fear not: for I have redeemed thee, I have called thee by thy name; thou art mine. When thou passest through the waters, I will be with thee; and through the rivers, they shall not overflow thee; when thou walkest through the fire, thou shalt not be burned; neither shall the flame kindle upon thee.

This verse paints a picture of fire and water that encompasses you on every side. Fire and water are both forces of destruction when uncontrolled. Walking through the fire and the water is an indication of pressure situations that you will experience in your daily walk. But pressure that is out of control to our natural human ability is still under God's control. God is not falling apart or losing control over the flood or fire we are walking through. God can keep you, protect you, and make you the winner over any and every situation—if you will trust in Him.

But what if you think it is all your fault? What if you think God is putting you through this pressure to punish you? What if you think God has abandoned you because you blew it? Then you will suffer through and allow that pressure to walk all over you. Jesus says be of "good cheer," He does not say to tough it out and hope you make it through the storm. We have to resist the devil in order for him to flee.

You have to allow the Word of God to develop an attitude in you. I mean an ATTITUDE! Have you ever had an attitude? God wants to give you one. When you allow Jesus and the Word to renew your mind (Romans 12:2), you will start thinking what God thinks. Jesus never allowed pressure to even phase Him. Jesus has an attitude when it comes to pressure, and He wants to develop this attitude in your spirit. Philippians 2:5 tells us to let the same attitude be in us that was in Jesus. So, what did Jesus do when pressure came against Him? He confronted and defeated it.

In Mark 4:35-41, we see a picture of Jesus confronting pressure that made everyone else fall apart. Jesus told His disciples, "Let us pass over unto the other side" (Mark 4: 35). He gave them faith-filled words on which to stand and build their resistance. But when the storm attacked their vessel, the disciples lost their cool. Now, I want to help you understand the brevity of their situation. Most of these men were fishermen who had spent their lives on boats in this body of water. They had been through some storms in their lifetime. Also, James and John—nicknamed the Sons of Thunder by Jesus in Mark 3:17—were on the boat. I don't picture them as being the wimpy type. The Amplified Bible describes this as a storm "of hurricane proportions" (Mark 4: 37 AMP). These guys weren't losing it over a little bit of thunder and lightening. Verse 37 tells us that the ship was full of water. The pressure was on! It looked like they were going under. To top it all off, Jesus was sleeping through it. Jesus was sound asleep amidst their shouting, the ship rocking back and forth, the clang of the buckets as they bailed water, and the howl of the wind. I'm telling you—Jesus was not moved by the pressure of the situation. Jesus had already spoken faith-filled words about this situation.

The disciples woke Him up with doubt in their mouths. "Don't you care that we are dying?" Now, that wasn't what Jesus had said. Jesus had said, "Let us pass over unto the other side." Look at the attitude Jesus had about the pressure. Pressure? No problem! Jesus rose above the circumstance and declared "Peace" to the problem.

Pressure cannot defeat an attitude of peace. Peace is a spiritual force that is only produced by abiding in the Word. Galatians 5:22 describes peace as a fruit that is produced in our spirits by the presence of the Word of God. This peace will surpass all your understanding of the situation. The disciples couldn't understand how Jesus could sleep through the storm. Jesus didn't understand why they were falling apart. Jesus says, "Why are you so fearful and how is it that you have no faith?" (Mark 4:40). In other words, "I gave you the same word to rest on that I was resting on. Why is your reaction so different than mine?" Those disciples could have stood up on the boat and shouted, "Jesus said we are going to the other side, so we are going over. We are not going under. Quit all this mess and be still." What do you think would have happened?

The bottom line is that God wants you to rise up and declare "peace" in the middle of the storm. He wants you to say what His Word says and act on what His Word says: God says that no weapon formed against you will prosper; God says you are more than a conqueror; God says that you are empowered to prosper in everything you put your hands to do. Stand up! Resist those thoughts of failure. "I am not going to fail! I will succeed! I am blessed in my marriage. I am blessed in my finances. I will not have a nervous breakdown! I have the mind of Christ. I will not be overcome by any disease. I will live and not die!" Speak the Word of God in the midst of your circumstance. Resist the pressure!

Resistance Against Your Progress to the Promise   8

Pressure attacks your vision—your ability to see clearly. The devil knows if he can steal your vision, he can steal your destiny. Destiny is your God-given destination—where God wants you to end up. If you can't see clearly where God wants you to go, you will never arrive where God wants you to be. God wants you to be in His land of promise. God wants you to be in the land of more than enough. Too many people have been blinded by pressure and cannot see God's promised land right in front of them. Destiny is in your face. Overcome the image that the devil is showing you and see what God sees.

Go with me to the day when God had brought His people to the edge of the land that He had promised to give them. In Numbers 13:2, God instructs Moses to send out representatives from each tribe to be witnesses to the land that He is giving to them.

Moses sends twelve men, but he gives instructions to them that weren't included in God's sightseeing itinerary. God didn't tell them to check out the people and see how strong they were. God didn't want them to evaluate the strength of the cities and determine whether or not they could handle a fight with them. God did not want them focusing on or considering those circumstances.

Being a pastor, this story reminds me that I must be very diligent to speak to my staff the exact instructions God has spoken and not include details that stem from my own concerns. Leaders are responsible for the direction and vision being broadcast from the pulpit. We must not allow our people's vision to be clouded by emotions, anxiety, or uncertainty. We must boldly declare

God's Word, even if our knees are knocking and our mind is saying, What if God doesn't come through? How do you think
Moses felt at that moment? Miriam and Aaron had just turned on
him. People had been complaining and carrying on throughout
this whole trip. "Moses brought us out here to die." "I wish I had
some leeks and garlic." "We were better off back in Egypt."
Everyone was critical of Moses and the job he was doing as pastor. The pressure was on Pastor Moses to get it right. Moses
allowed this pressure to poison his vision. When Moses' vision
was polluted, the pollution ran down into his staff because he
instructed them to look for trouble where there was none.

The twelve-man entourage stepped into a land that God had
promised to give to them. They saw that the land was good. They
tasted the fruit and drank the clean water. For forty days they
experienced the abundance and beauty of the land God had
sworn to give them. As they journeyed back to camp, they even
carried evidence of what God had spoken: a cluster of grapes so
huge that it required two men to carry.

But ten of the men returned with distorted vision. They
returned with a report of strong people, walled cities, and giants
in the land. These are exactly the things that Moses told them to
be on the watch for. If you look for trouble, you will find it.
Because of pressure, their ability to see clearly was hindered. They
could not see the vision that God had for them.

What caused two of them, Joshua and Caleb, to see this situation so vastly different than the others? They were seeing clearly
what God had said. They had God's vision. They were seeing the
situation through the filter of the Word of God. When I read this
passage, I can feel the frustration in Joshua and Caleb as they
implore the people to see what God said. "Can't you see what I
see? It's as plain as day! Man, it is right in front of your face! Can't
you see it?" The Bible says that Joshua and Caleb were so upset by
the doubt and unbelief that was coming out of people's mouth
that they tore and ripped their clothes.

God also had something to say about the people's response.
He didn't baby or coddle them. God said, "How long will it be

before you believe me?" (Numbers 14:11). If we could just recognize that pressure comes to steal the Word from our heart before it can take root and grow into faith, then we would be more diligent when it comes to believing. The only responsibility that was required of the Israelites was to believe. Think about all they had witnessed up to this point. God kept them through the plagues that devastated Egypt. He brought them out of bondage, with payment in full for their years of labor. God led them by fire and cloud, divided the Red Sea, and provided manna from heaven and water from a rock. What more does it take to prove that God will do what He said He will do? All they had to do was say, "Pressure? No Problem! God said this land is ours—giants and all. So what if they have walled cities? We have God's Word!"

God expects you and I to have the same respect for the power of the Word of God that He does. God knows the integrity and ability of the Word that He speaks. We are desensitized by a society that says what it does not mean. "That burns me up." "I thought I would die." "I'm dying to go." We use words in a flippant, nonchalant attitude.

We also make promises and break them at a moment's notice. "Well, I know I told you I would be available to help, but I just can't make it." We are only as honorable as our word. Because we don't honor our word, we expect that God won't honor His. God designed the family to prepare children for obedience to God's Word. We do our children an injustice by teaching them that we don't mean what we say. Children are supposed to learn respect for God's Word by being taught respect for our words. "Now, I mean it! If you do that one more time…" "I'm not telling you again!" "What did I say?" "Didn't I tell you…" Yes, you told them, but they didn't believe you because you never showed them any power behind your words.

God had continually revealed to His people that His Word was true and full of integrity. Notice that they had been raised under the influence of Pharaoh, who constantly said what He did not mean. Under pressure of the plagues, Pharaoh would agree to let the people go. Once the pressure of a plague was eased, he refused to honor his word. God's people had been governed, for years, by a leader with no integrity in his word; therefore, they acted like God wouldn't honor His Word.

The Bible clearly states, "The fear of the Lord is the beginning of wisdom" (Psalm 111:10a). To respect and revere the Lord, we must have respect and reverence for His Word. God meant what He said and said what He meant. God had given His Word about the Promised Land, but they didn't believe Him. What an insult! That is exactly what pressure wanted to accomplish!

Look at the pattern of pressure. Pressure on Moses affected his staff. Pressure on the staff affected the whole church. The report of ten men hindered God's vision and disqualified those who succumbed to it from receiving God's promise. Pressure is not out to stop only you. It is out for your family, your job, your church, and God's vision for your life. Pressure wants to stop your progress to God's promise.

The Pressure of "Not Enough" 9

Financial pressure is prevalent in our society today. From the pressure of "not enough" to the pressure of "keeping up with the Joneses," people are fighting the worry, fear, and anxiety associated with finances. "How are we going to make it?" "How can we possibly tithe and still buy groceries?" "Why are we fighting such a financial battle?" This chapter will help you identify and alleviate this pressure.

It is a necessity for the believer to abandon the system of the world and enter into God's system of finances. This change begins with our thinking. In God's system, I am not the owner—He is. I have become steward or manager over the resources of my life—my time, my family, my body, my possessions—all that I have is God's. I am not my own. I am bought with a price (see I Corinthians 6:19-20).

As I change my thinking, I change my strategy. Instead of trying to just get by, I am now strategizing to build and better God's kingdom (see Matthew 6:33). I begin to study God's method for kingdom business. I build my faith to know that God's will for my life is to prosper in all that I set my hand to do (see III John 2). I see that He will increase me more and more (see Psalm 115:14) and that God wants abundance and no lack in my life.

Victory over financial pressure begins within us. We often expect God to fix our finances by dropping a large sum of money in our laps. Instead, God gives a word: Luke 6:38.

Give and it shall be given unto you, good measure, pressed down and shaken together and running over.

God's kingdom is a kingdom of seedtime and harvest. God provides us with seeds to deposit in our hearts—seeds that produce a harvest of financial strength. We have to quit looking for a "get rich quick" prayer and understand that God wants to produce a constant flow of provision in our lives.

The plan that Jesus has for our lives is to establish and build a foundation of abundance in our hearts. For this plan to be set in motion in your life, you must allow the Word to rearrange your thinking, priorities, and attitudes. Does it sound easy? Well, it isn't easy on your flesh. As a matter of fact, changing your priorities and attitudes can become quite uncomfortable.

Let's investigate God's Word in Judges 6.

> *And the children of Israel did evil in the sight of the Lord: and the Lord delivered them into the hand of Midian seven years. And the hand of Midian prevailed against Israel: and because of the Midianites the children of Israel made them the dens which are in the mountains, and caves, and strong holds. And so it was, when Israel had sown, that the Midianites came up, and the Amalekites, and the children of the east, even they came up against them; And they encamped against them, and destroyed the increase of the earth, till thou come unto Gaza, and left no sustenance for Israel, neither sheep, nor ox, nor ass. For they came up with their cattle and their tents, and they came as grasshoppers for multitude; for both they and their camels were without number: and they entered into the land to destroy it. And Israel was greatly impoverished because of the Midianites; and the children of Israel cried unto the Lord.* Judges 6:1-6

How do you deal with pressure in the presence of a problem? Personally, I always wanted God to get me out of my mess and then teach me how to change. He never chose to do it my way. Thankfully, I finally chose to do things His way. That is what happens in Judges 6 in the life of Gideon and the children of Israel.

The actions and behaviors of God's people were not those pre-scribed by God (vs. 1). They did evil in the sight of the Lord.

Let's consider some financial choices we might make. What if our choice to pay everything else first and choose to pay tithe last—if there is any left—is against God's plan? What if choosing to spend more than we make, using credit cards as "faith proj-ects," is against God's instruction for our finances? What if our financial decisions are ruled by our senses and not God's Word? What if we make Jesus Lord in every area of our lives except for the area of our finances? Would any of those "what ifs" be consid-ered evil in the sight of the Lord? Yes! Evil in the Lord's sight can be something other than what we consider blatant sin. To do evil in the sight of the Lord is to be disobedient to His Word in any area.

The story in Judges 6 begins by giving us an understanding of what caused the problems in the Israelites' lives. God is never our problem. God is always our solution. He isn't trying to destroy you. But He won't force anything on you—not even victory. The Lord delivered the children of Israel into the hand of Midian for seven years. If you keep resisting His instructions, God will throw up His hands and let you disobey your way right into misery. He will nudge you to turn away from disaster, but He won't stand in your way.

God's people resorted to living in caves and hiding in the mountains because of their adversity. Pressure drove them to a place God never intended for them to be. God opened the Red Sea, brought water from a rock, and stopped the sun from setting to bring this people from bondage into this land of plenty. He didn't exert all of that effort to have His people holed up in an animal's den because of an enemy.

By reading verses 3 through 6, we can identify this enemy—lack, poverty, not enough. The seed sown (v. 3) became the tar-get: not their children, not their wives, not their livestock—their seed. Isn't that just like the devil? His MO (method of operation) is to steal, kill, and destroy. In the parable of the sower, Jesus tells us about seed that is stolen, seed that is killed, and seed that is destroyed. If your adversary can stop your seed, it will affect your children, your marriage, and every other part of your life.

Verse 4 describes how "they destroyed the increase of the earth" and "left no sustenance for Israel." This is a disturbing illustration of how "not enough" devastates a person's life. What a miserable feeling it is to pour your life into something, day in and day out, and have nothing to show for it at the end of the week, the end of the month, or even the end of your life. The Israelites invested their best seed, their time, and all of their energy into the ground. Perhaps you have invested the best years of your life and your greatest resources and you still see no results. Well, then, let's dig deeper.

God's covenant is specifically designed to cover our seedtime and harvest. Harvest will never reach full potential outside of God's covenant. First of all, our Heavenly Father is the ultimate harvester. John 15:1 clearly tells us this:

I am the true vine, and my Father is the husbandman.

Deuteronomy 28:1-6 promises that when we obey God's instructions our harvest will receive God's empowerment to prosper.

And it shall come to pass, if thou shalt hearken diligently unto the voice of the Lord thy God, to observe and to do all his commandments which I command thee this day, that the Lord thy God will set thee on high above all nations of the earth: And all these blessings shall come on thee, and over- take thee, if thou shalt hearken unto the voice of the Lord thy God. Blessed shalt thou be in the city, and blessed shalt thou be in the field. Blessed shall be the fruit of thy body, and the fruit of thy ground, and the fruit of thy cattle, the increase of thy kine, and the flocks of thy sheep. Blessed shall be thy basket and thy store. Blessed shalt thou be when thou comest in, and blessed shalt thou be when thou goest out.

God's covenant is the only equipment that is qualified to defend our seed. The people had thrown away the only weapon that could stop the seed-eater. Malachi 3:11 calls it the devourer. In this scripture, God promises to rebuke the seed-eater so that "he will not destroy the fruits of your ground." God, also, has the power to ensure that your "vine will not cast her fruit before the time in the field" (Malachi 3:11). I call that power to protect my harvest.

God's design for our lives is that we are fruitful in what we do. Third John 2 shows God's desire for us to prosper or succeed in reaching. "Not enough" is a blight on God's covenant people. Ezekiel 36:30 says that famine was a reproach.

And I will multiply the fruit of the tree, and the increase of the field, that ye shall receive no more reproach of famine among the heathen.

Instead, God wants to work His covenant in our lives to produce the following results:

For the seed shall be prosperous; the vine shall give her fruit, and the ground shall give her increase, and the heavens shall give their dew; and I will cause the remnant of this people to possess all these things. And it shall come to pass, that as ye were a curse among the heathen, O house of Judah, and house of Israel; so will I save you, and ye shall be a blessing: fear not, but let your hands be strong.
Zechariah 8:12-13

Life as the Israelites knew it in Judges 6 was a far cry from this. Lack, poverty, and "not enough" had invaded their lives in a drastic way. When the pressure became too much for them to handle, they finally resorted to reaching for God. Why do we try everything else first and save His help as a last resort? Let me encourage you: Don't wait until the pressure of "not enough" is so present in your life that your children feel it and your marriage is breaking under the strain. Run to God at the first sign of your seed being destroyed.

My encouraging instructions are not based on a testimony I read in someone else's book. Of all the pressures I have encountered in my Christian life, "not enough" was by far the worst! Perhaps that is why this chapter is longer than the others. When you read my life story (Chapter 15), you will know that my life before God was a mess. It is understandable why I had so much heartache in a lifestyle of sin. Jesus and I had some long talks about why financial struggles were present in my life after coming to Him. Since that time, I have encountered many people who asked the same questions that I asked, "If I made so much money serving sin, why am I so broke serving God?" (Of course, I never seemed to keep any of the money I made serving sin.)

I want to help you find your way free of this financial pressure.

God looks for people who are working for a harvest even in the most severe of circumstances. Gideon—whose name means "warrior, one who cuts down or destroys,"—was threshing wheat in the winepress to hide it from the Midianites. An angel of the Lord appeared to Gideon and announced, "The Lord is with thee, thou mighty man of valor [fearless courage]" (Judges 6:12). Hello! Excuse me, Lord! The guy is hiding in the winepress. He isn't defending the country or showing any bravery. He is hiding from the enemy. When God brings a solution, He isn't moved by your present situation.

God isn't moved by your present perception, either. Gideon has a "not enough" mentality. Look at his response to every declaration that the Lord makes over him. First, the word of the Lord is, "The Lord is with thee, thou mighty man of valor." Gideon responds with, "If the Lord is with us, why...?" (Judges 6:13). Second, the Lord says, "Go in this thy might, and thou shalt save Israel from the hand of the Midianites, have not I sent thee?" (Judges 6:14). Gideon responds, "How can I deliver Israel?" (Judges 6:15). He is still seeing empty when God says he is full. Finally, God says, "Surely I will be with you and you shall..." (Judges 6:16).

Gideon, still grasping to visualize what God is saying, responds, "If now I have found grace in thy sight, then show me a sign that thou talkest with me" (Judges 6:17). He wants a sign to prove that they are having a conversation? Lord, help us!

In Chapter 3, we investigated perception and in Chapter 7 we discussed attitude. These subjects are closely related, and I want to zone in on one of them. Attitude is a way of behaving or a manner of carrying one's self, indicative of mood or condition. While attitude does reflect the state of mind, attitude displays outwardly what you are perceiving inwardly. We could consider attitude as "stage two" of what is being birthed in our perception.

To solve the problems in your life, you will need two things:

1. The right attitude
2. The right plan of action

Gideon obviously needed the right attitude. This was the purpose of the conversation between Gideon and the angel of the Lord. The only way for God to develop His attitude within our hearts is through His Word. Gideon needed to change his outlook on the problem he was facing. You have to do the same thing! Change your attitude. Adopt God's attitude. It will make the difference between winning and losing.

Next, God instructed Gideon to set some things in order. While I will go deeper in explaining the power of order in our next chapter, I would like to examine a few points about order as it pertains to Gideon and "not enough." Let's look at verses 25 and 26 of Judges 6:

And it came to pass the same night, that the Lord said unto him, Take thy father's young bullock, even the second bullock of seven years old, and throw down the altar of Baal that thy father hath, and cut down the grove that is by it: And build an altar unto the Lord thy God upon the top of this rock, in the ordered place, and take the second bullock, and offer a burnt sacrifice with the wood of the grove which thou shalt cut down.

In verse 26, the phrase "in the ordered place" could also be defined as "in an orderly manner." Notice that God instructs the enemy's structure to be torn down and God's structure to be built in a specific orderly fashion. There are financial mindsets and structures that you may be operating in that God wants you to tear down. Have you ever stopped to investigate why you do what you do? Why do you put five dollars in the offering plate on Sunday and two on Wednesday? Why do you tithe after you have paid the other bills first? Why do you always have time to watch television and hardly find time to pray? Why do you know the statistics of your favorite pitcher but you don't know the title of your pastor's latest sermon series?

God will require you to put your life in the order directed by His Word. Tithe the right way. Talk the right way. Act right. Live right. Determine to tear down any habits you developed that are built contrary to God's instruction. When Gideon obeyed God, his obedience positioned him to receive the right plan of action. Victory over "not enough" will never be released into the hands of the disobedient. God enacted His plan through Gideon, and the entire country overcame the pressure of "not enough." Imagine what will happen as you overcome lack and enable others to go free.

The Right Plan of Action: Get Things in Order

Having discussed pressure's intent, let's now investigate some strategies for pressure-proofing our lives. Pressure generally comes disguised in a problem. It is when the problems pile up and pressure increases that we tend to become weary in doing what is right. So how do we avoid this pile up? Prepare the right plan of action. Reacting to the problem always puts us on the defensive instead of the offensive. In order for you to gain ground, you have to be running with the ball. God's plan of action will give you the home-field advantage, and you can be prepared for every step of the way.

In Judges 4, Deborah has been placed in a position of leadership as a judge over Israel. Deborah's name comes from the root word dabar, meaning "to arrange, to speak, or to subdue." Through speaking, Deborah would arrange and subdue the problems that were brought to her. God also arranged our world and everything that pertains to it by speaking (see Hebrews 11:3). In Genesis 1, "And God said" is written ten times. God put the universe in order by speaking faith-filled words and arranging it how He wanted it. Furthermore, as God dealt with the sin of Adam and Eve, He dealt with the problem by speaking the answer (see Genesis 3:15).

My favorite passage to illustrate dabar is found in Jeremiah:

Then said I, Ah, Lord God! behold, I cannot speak [dabar]: for I am a child. But the Lord said unto me, Say not, I am a child: for thou shalt go to all that I shall send thee, and whatsoever I command thee thou shalt speak

[dabar]. Be not afraid of their faces: for I am with thee to
deliver thee, saith the Lord. Then the Lord put forth his
hand, And touched my mouth. And the Lord said unto
me, Behold, I have put my words in thy mouth. See, I have
this day set thee over the nations and over the kingdoms,
to root out, and to pull down, and to destroy, and to throw
down, to build, and to plant. Jeremiah 1:6-10

Jeremiah says to God, "I cannot speak-arrange, subdue, and
put in order." But God says, "Don't dabar that! That is not what I
want you to establish in your future. You will go and you will
speak—arrange, subdue, and put in order—what I say." At the
end of verse 9 we see the key to dabar. God puts His words in our
mouths to produce the effect described in verse 10: to root out,
pull down, destroy, throw down, build, and plant. As we speak
God's Word into our circumstances, it goes into our problems
and destroys or throws them down. Then, as we continue speaking, the Word begins to build and plant what God desires in our
life.

So shall my word be that goeth forth out of my mouth: it
shall not return unto me void, but it shall accomplish that
which I please, and it shall prosper in the thing whereto I
sent it. Isaiah 55:11

The word "prosper" here means "to push forward, break out,
come mightily, go over, and cause to prosper." If you were to
replace "thing" with "problem" in this verse, you could say that
God's Word will push forward, break out, come mightily against,
and go over the problem that you send it to.

What are we waiting for? Dabar! Let's get God's Word in our
mouths and put pressure in its rightful place. Speak to your problems. Speak to your future. Speak to your finances. Speak to your
health. God says SPEAK!

Deborah was named according to her character. Keep that in
mind as we go deeper into her story.

And Deborah, a prophetess, the wife of Lapidoth, she judged Israel at that time. And she dwelt under the palm tree of Deborah between Ramah and Bethel in mount Ephraim: and the children of Israel came up to her for judgment. And she sent and called Barak the son of Abinoam out of Kedeshnaphtali, and said unto him, Hath not the Lord God of Israel commanded, saying, Go and draw toward mount Tabor, and take with thee ten thousand men of the children of Naphtali and of the children of Zebulun? And I will draw unto thee to the river Kishon Sisera, the captain of Jabin's army, with his chariots and his multitude; and I will deliver him into thine hand. And Barak said unto her, If thou wilt go with me, then I will go: but if thou wilt not go with me, then I will not go. And she said, I will surely go with thee: notwithstanding the journey that thou takest shall not be for thine honour; for the Lord shall sell Sisera into the hand of a woman. And Deborah arose, and went with Barak to Kedesh.

Judges 4:4-9

Deborah takes her position under a palm tree. The Hebrew word for "palm tree" means "to stand erect." The palm tree is a sign of strength in adversity; in winds of hurricane proportions, the palm tree can bend under the pressure and not break. Deborah's palm tree of choice was planted between Ramah (height) and Bethel (house of God). She stood tall in the house of God and gained her strength from being in her God-given place. Ephraim means "fruitfulness" or "double fruit." Deborah is in a mountain of fruitfulness; she takes her place to arrange and put in order situations in the lives of God's people.

From verse 3, we learn that the children of Israel were experiencing miserable oppression from Jabin, king of Canaan, for twenty years. They began crying out to God. Because of these prayers, God speaks to Barak a plan to defeat pressure. The Lord always has a plan to overcome pressure in your life. God gave Barak a Word on which to establish his victory. Because Barak had neglected to rehearse God's Word to himself, he lacked the courage to face the pressure of the situation.

How many times have you been between that proverbial "rock and a hard place," begging God to intervene on your behalf, all the while knowing what He said about your predicament. After God says it, He wants you to say it! God sends Deborah to Barak, and what does she do? She says what God said! Barak decided, "I'm not going unless you go with me." In other words, "I'm not facing this pressure without the ability to speak what God said and arrange my victory." And it is not saying it one time that brings victory. You have to keep speaking all the way to victory.

Deborah was speaking the end from the beginning by saying what God said. She understood that if she was the one—the vessel—releasing the commands of God, then the victory over pressure was coming forth out of her mouth. Deborah stepped into battle already victorious because she put the problem in its place. Deborah set things in order—God's Word is on top; pressure is underneath.

We position ourselves by speaking doubt, speaking faith or not speaking at all. When we speak doubt, or speak as if the problem is insurmountable, we are giving the problem the place of authority in our lives. We arrange the problem in a position of having advantage over us.

When we speak what God said, we place God's Word in the place of authority over pressure, problems, and circumstances. We arrange and subdue the problem under God's Word, and the Word has advantage over pressure.

When we don't say anything, we leave the positioning and placement of our circumstances to the "wind." Say, for instance, you have a fertile piece of ground and you want a garden to grow on it. But, you choose not to plant any seeds; you are going to just hope that what you want comes up. You may want tomatoes, corn, and green beans, but you haven't planted anything. You will end up with weeds and crabgrass. The wind will determine what grows in your garden because it will blow all kinds of unwanted seed into your ground. Your mouth will determine what your future will harvest. Proverbs 13:2 says, "A man shall eat good by the fruit of his mouth."

The children of Israel give us an example to consider. As they were on their way to the Promised Land, they continuously spoke against what God said. "It would have been better for us to stay in Egypt than to die in the wilderness. You have brought us forth into this wilderness, to kill us all with hunger" (see Exodus 14:11; 16:3). They did end up dying in the wilderness—not because it was God's will for their life, but because they spoke what pressure was telling them to say.

Pressure is not the final authority in your life! Circumstances are not the final authority in your life! Situations are not in control! Declare that Jesus is Lord over every area of your life. Jesus is the final authority in every situation. God's Word is truth. Facts don't change truth. Truth changes fact. Attack the facts of your circumstance with the truth of God's Word.

11 The Focus of Faith

To overcome and defeat pressure in our lives, we must focus our faith. Faith is the victory that overcomes the world, and God has given to every man the measure of faith. Faith is the substance of things hoped for and the evidence of things not seen (see Hebrews 11:1). So, how do we harness and utilize this powerful force of faith? Focus is the harness for faith.

In II Kings 4, we see a perfect illustration of focused faith. A woman who lived in Shunem noticed Elisha and "constrained him to eat bread" (II Kings 4:8). This woman took notice of the presence of God upon Elisha and said to her husband, "I perceive that this is a holy man of God" (II Kings 4:9). In Bible times, a man of God represented to the people the Word of God. Proper perception prompted this woman to continue in her relationship with the Word, and soon she had prepared room for the Word to take a position of prominence in her life. As we perceive the presence of God in His Word, we will move our schedule and comforts to make room for God.

As the woman from Shunem honored the Word in her life, the Word blessed her in return. When the man of God spoke from his lips the desire of her heart, she grabbed that Word with all sincerity and said, "Do not lie unto thine handmaid" (II Kings 4:16). In other words, "I am receiving this as a Word from God. Don't mess with my dreams. You'd better be telling me the truth because if you say it, I'll dare to believe it."

Nine months later she gave birth to the desire of her heart. That child was a covenant completion. This woman had a covenant right to "be fruitful and multiply" (Genesis 1:28). Her focus on God's Word produced peace—nothing missing, nothing broken—in her covenant.

There came a day when pressure attacked her covenant. Her son—the desire of her heart, her covenant completion—came in the house and, after laying his head upon her lap, died. Let's talk about "Pressure? No problem!" now. Just how do you handle the pressure of a dead-end situation? How do you deal with a circumstance that appears lifeless and without hope? You deal with it in the same way Abraham dealt with his lifeless situation, the same way Jesus faced the tomb of Lazarus, the same way God raised Jesus from the dead: You focus your faith on God's Word.

Notice how the woman from Shunem dealt with her circumstance. She didn't wail, moan, or begin to mourn. She didn't alert the family or spread the news. She carried the child up to the place where the man of God had spoken the Word of God concerning this promise to her. This was the room and abode she had prepared for God and His Word. This was the contact to the covenant.

In the midst of a crisis, we must cling to the stability of God's Word. There is nothing in the entire universe more stable than the Word. We take for granted that whenever we look up the sky will be there or whenever we take a step the ground will hold us. But God's Word is even more trustworthy than the heavens or the earth.

Heaven and earth will pass away, but My words will by no means pass away. Matthew 24:35 NKJV

As the woman from Shunem goes to her husband and requests a donkey, her husband questions, "Why are you going to see the preacher? It's not Sunday or Wednesday" (II Kings 4:23). With deliberate focus on her outcome, she declares a one-word response that in the Hebrew language speaks volumes: "Shalom!" She opens her mouth and dabars that she has nothing missing, nothing broken. She wasn't denying her problem or living a fantasy. She was applying the pressure of her covenant against the pressure of her circumstance. She knew who gave her that child. She knew who made it possible for her to birth that son. Her answer was a focused faith declaration: "I have the peace that comes from being made whole! I am not missing or broken in this circumstance." That is what shalom means.

> *Let us hold fast the profession of our faith without waver-ing; [for he is faithful that promised].* Hebrews 10:23

Too often, we give up instead of holding on. How many vic-tories would never have been celebrated if the victors had given up? Victory didn't come easy to Moses. David had to face the challenge. Gideon had to get over it. Abraham had to speak things that were not as though they were. Samson had to face his mis-takes. Esther had to take her place. Job had to get his mouth right. Noah had to build his boat. Isaac had to sow in the time of famine. The Hebrew boys had to walk through the fire. Daniel faced the den of lions. Joseph endured the pit and the prison to get to the palace. So why are you giving up? God is faithful, but you have to hold fast!

The woman from Shunem neared the place where the man of God was and he sent his servant to ask her, "Shalom with you? Shalom with your husband? Shalom with the child?" Her response to the servant was the same focused faith as before: "I have the peace that comes from being made whole!" As she fell at the prophet's feet, she held onto her profession of faith without waver-ing and reminded him of the Word she had been given. Elisha instructed his servant to go, but she was determined that he would come and change this situation. That is the kind of determination we must develop. Focused, determined faith in God and the ability of His Word will overcome every attack sent to destroy us.

The Shunammite woman spoke her end from the beginning. She held fast to her profession of faith and focused her belief. The pressure of the circumstances could not withstand focused faith, and death gave way to life. Nothing is impossible for God, and all things are possible to him that believes.

This woman's story is an inspiration for me. Her tenacity stirs me up. I can connect with her determination partly because of my own experience. I became pregnant with my third child, Angela Lavayne Steele, in 1994, while Philip and I were still recovering from the pain of miscarrying a child and all the "what ifs" that go with it. We determined to be vigilant, understanding that our adversary was seeking to devour our seed. We spoke the Word over our baby. I rejected the thoughts of fear and worry that came into my mind. What if you lose this baby, too? What if you miscarry again? We prayed; we believed. We quit arguing because we felt that had been an avenue the devil had used to destroy our first child. (We were very carnal in those early days of our marriage.)

Everything seemed perfect. Angela was a good weight and a healthy size. She was born right on schedule. But, when the doctors held her up, she was blue. They put her under the oxygen, and she returned to a healthy pink—but only for a moment. My husband held her momentarily, then the doctors quietly took her from the room. It took a few minutes for it to register that things weren't normal. We were calling the family to announce her arrival when I asked the nurses, "When will they bring the baby back? Why is it taking them so long to weigh her? Where is my baby?" I wasn't getting a definite answer. Instead, I was getting that evasive answer that sends your internal alarm system into emergency mode.

The doctor came in to speak with Philip and me. Philip reached for my hand, and we held each other tightly. I distinctly remember bracing myself not to agree with the doctor's report or show any fear about what she said. She told us their prognosis, "Angela has a punctured lung and possibly a heart condition. We will have to transport her to the children's hospital in Kansas City." After the doctor left the room, we began to pray. I remember the scripture that we stood on.

He shall not be afraid of evil tidings: his heart is fixed, trusting in the Lord. Psalm 112:7

We fixed our hearts and refused to lose our baby. We declared, "Angela will live and not die and declare the works of the Lord!" From across the room, the television that had been left on began preaching faith as evangelist Kenneth Copeland's daily broadcast began. God equipped us to defeat and overcome the devourer with focused faith.

My husband followed the ambulance that carried my covenant completion to the children's hospital. As she lay under a plastic oxygen tent struggling for each breath, he laid hands on that plastic and declared, "You will live and not die! By His stripes you are healed!" Doctors contemplated inserting a tube into her chest. They ran tests on her heart and lungs. But, Angela started getting better. Her punctured lung healed on its own—without any tubes in her chest. The doctors were amazed at her quick recovery. We weren't amazed. We expected our shalom—nothing missing, nothing broken. We expected the peace that comes from having our daughter alive and well, because God is faithful when we hold fast against the pressure.

Faith vs. Pressure 12

In the previous chapter, we studied the focus of faith. Let's go deeper in our understanding of the dynamics of applying faith against the pressure. To demonstrate these faith dynamics, we will look at Mark 5:24-34.

And Jesus went with him; and much people followed him, and thronged him. And a certain woman, which had an issue of blood twelve years, And had suffered many things of many physicians, and had spent all that she had, and was nothing bettered, but rather grew worse, When she had heard of Jesus, came in the press behind, and touched his garment. For she said, If I may touch but his clothes, I shall be whole. And straightway the fountain of her blood was dried up; and she felt in her body that she was healed of that plague. And Jesus, immediately knowing in himself that virtue had gone out of him, turned him about in the press, and said, Who touched my clothes? And his disciples said unto him, Thou seest the multitude thronging thee, and sayest thou, Who touched me? And he looked round about to see her that had done this thing. But the woman fearing and trembling, knowing what was done in her, came and fell down before him, and told him all the truth. And he said unto her, Daughter, thy faith hath made thee whole; go in peace, and be whole of thy plague.

There is more to faith and more to believing than just saying your confession and standing against the obstacle. Many people see the exterior actions of faith and try to duplicate those actions. Just because someone else gave away their house or car doesn't mean that if you give yours away God will replace it. We can't operate on foolishness or presumption and get the results of faith. We have to check and double-check, "Am I in faith? Am I thinking, speaking, and acting in faith?" When a pilot is preparing for take off, he checks and double checks his instruments. Is that the last time he ever checks those instruments? No, that pilot is constantly watching those instruments to make sure the plane is on target for its destination. Course adjustments may be necessary along the way. Check your spirit. Are you in faith?

The woman in Mark 5 had clearly endured the pressure of her situation for a long time. Twelve years of physical illness had taken their toll on her body, her relationships, and her social life. In her condition, she was prohibited to engage in normal social activities. Her condition kept her from going to church. She was not allowed within a certain distance of the rabbi or priest. She was labeled by society as "unclean" and had to proclaim that label every time she stepped out of her house.

Her condition had continually grown worse. She had spent all that she had, to no avail. The word "spent" in verse 26 comes from a root word that means "to devour." In Luke 8:43, the word used for spent comes from the root word that means "to destroy." Any time we see that someone is "spent"—physically, emotionally, or financially—we should recognize that it fits the devil's MO (method of operation). He is constantly seeking to destroy or devour.

Pressure was slowly squeezing the life out of this woman. Her life was clearly descending, destined for death. But after twelve years of this condition, the course of her life was altered. What changed the course of her life? What caused her direction to be changed? Verse 27 holds the key to the change in her direction: "When she had heard of Jesus." Hearing the Word is the beginning of victory. There is no lasting victory without the Word. I John 5:4 says that faith is the victory that overcomes the world. The faith to overcome enters our hearts by way of our hearing.

Faith comes by hearing and hearing by the Word of God.
Romans 10:17

God created you to operate and function in this world as a faith being. You were designed to receive words, deposit them in your heart, and release the power held in those words. More specifically, God designed you to receive His Word, build a treasure of His Words in your heart, and release the power of His life into your heart and out of your mouth.

Words are like capsules; they carry power in them. Proverbs tells us that the power of life and death are in the tongue, where words are formed. Think about this practical illustration. When you say spiteful things in a heated argument, call a person names, or tell someone you don't love them anymore, you are inflicting injury that does not easily go away. Why is it that an argument can be so painful? In the years of my life B.C. (before Christ), I had some outrageous arguments, the kind you could hear down the block. I can remember saying to my late husband, "I'd rather you take your fist and hit me than to run your mouth at me like that." He usually ended up giving me my wish. The fact was it hurt worse to hear those awful things and it took longer to heal from those verbal wounds than the busted eardrum or cracked jaw. Words carry power.

Take, for instance, a young child. You can speak words of encouragement and confidence to that child and empower him with self-esteem. That child can face challenges in life with a strong mental attitude because you have released words of love and assurance into his heart. But what happens to the child who suffers constant verbal abuse? If you degrade or insult a child— "You are so clumsy!" "Come here, brat." "Stupid kid. You are a bad girl!" "What a mean little boy!"—you are releasing the power to fail into that heart. Words carry power.

Satan knows how we were created. Although he has no power to create, he takes our power to release the power of life and death and subtly uses it against us. For example, our society today uses words and sayings that make our grandparents blush. People who lived 150 years ago would be appalled at the language on television and in schools today. Look at some of the things the devil has taught people to say: "That tickles me to death!" "I laughed till I died." "That burns me up." "That scared me to death." And on and on it goes. People are releasing power through their words that they don't want working in their life.

What is God's plan? Hear God's Word. Do God's Word. Speak God's Word. Focus on God's Word. Meditate on God's Word. Release the power contained in God's Word into your life. That is what God intended—and still intends—to be our method of operation in this earth.

The woman is Mark chapter 5 who had an issue of blood is an example of this. When she heard the Word, her actions and her words were changed. Why? The power of the Word (that is, Jesus; see John 1:1) went in her ears, through her mind, and into her heart. In her heart, the Word released God's power to change her mind, words, and actions; thus, she was able to reach and embrace the healing and wholeness available for her.

How did her heart release the power of God's Word? Your heart is like the engine of a car. Your car takes gasoline—the fuel—and processes that fuel in an engine. The engine processes that gasoline and releases a force of energy that propels the car. The gasoline by itself is not the power. You can carry that gasoline down the road, but it is not going to get you to your destination any quicker. Gasoline requires an engine to release its power. God created your physical body in the same manner. Your body requires fuel—food and water—to function. Upon receiving that fuel, your body automatically breaks it down and releases the energy contained in that food. Some food has more nutritional energy than others. You don't get the same amount of energy out of potato chips as you do a bowl of Wheaties.

Based on these analogies, think about your spirit or your heart. Your heart takes in whatever fuel you are providing for it. Are you filling up with God's Word or the circumstances of the world? Your car doesn't get full unless you take it the station and pay the price to fill it up. Your spirit doesn't get full unless you take it to the Word and pay the price of your time to fill it up.

Once you deposit the fuel in your spiritual tank, your heart goes to work releasing power based on the fuel you put in. If you have filled your tank with junk or nonsense, like news reports or media hype you will get little or no force of faith. You may even be releasing a force of fear. But if you fill up with God's Word, you will always release a force of faith.

This force of faith is not designed to remain in your engine. Just like you put your car in gear and step on the accelerator, you must put your mind in gear and release faith through your actions and your mouth.

Let's talk about the actions first. The woman in Mark 5 came out of the house to which she had been restricted for years and approached Jesus, who was known as a rabbi and teacher. She dared to come near, even though Jairus, a ruler of the synagogue was there next to Jesus. Her actions were in line with her mind and her heart. The power released in her heart was "I shall be whole." This power flowed to her mind, "I shall be whole." Her mind engaged the required actions: Touch His clothes to be made whole. Her faith was in gear, and her actions were in line with faith.

Sometimes I find that heart is filled with faith but I am stuck in idle. That is why I say to ask yourself, "Am I in faith?" In Acts 14, Paul was preaching to a man who had never walked; he had no strength or ability in his feet. The man heard Paul preach, and Paul recognized that he had faith to be healed. But he was still lame. His heart was filling up with faith; he just needed to put his mind in gear with his heart and act on his faith.

The woman in Mark 5 heard the Word, which deposited faith in her heart. She had to engage her mind and her mouth for the force of faith to propel her to wholeness. Her actions and her words were corresponding, not conflicting. Don't let your mouth put the brakes on your actions. You can talk yourself right out of gas and find yourself stranded halfway to your victory.

When verse 28 says, "For she said," it implies that she kept on saying. Do you remember the children's story The Little Engine That Could? The little engine was speaking the end from the beginning. He was keeping his mouth in line with his heart. That is what this woman was doing. She kept releasing the power in her heart, and it went back in her ears and back into her heart. Not only was she keeping her faith focused—like the Shunammite woman and like Deborah—but she was acting like God, who calls those things that are not as though they were.

Check and see: Are you in faith? Is your tank full? Are you in gear with your mind to release faith in your actions and your words? It's time to inspect our instruments. We are preparing for take off.

Praise vs. Pressure 13

Praising God is a way to release the force of faith stored in your heart. God designed praise to aid in our victory over pressure. Praise creates an atmosphere for God's presence. While we know that God dwells inside of us as born-again believers, the atmosphere around us needs to be filled with His presence as well.

> Make a joyful noise unto the Lord, all ye lands. Serve the Lord with gladness: come before his presence with singing. Know ye that the Lord he is God: it is he that hath made us, and not we ourselves; we are his people, and the sheep of his pasture. Enter into his gates with thanksgiving, and into his courts with praise: be thankful unto him, and bless his name. For the Lord is good; his mercy is everlasting; and his truth endureth to all generations. Psalms 100:1-5

This psalm illustrates an attitude of praise that God desires us to live in. This attitude of praise helps us recognize the presence of our supernatural God. When the words of praise come out of your lips, they charge the atmosphere with expectancy and faith. When words of worry, anxiety, and frustration, which are products of pressure, come out of our mouth, the atmosphere is heavy with doubt. Have you ever walked into a room where two people had been arguing just moments before? The tension in the air caused by their words is evident. That is one example of how our atmosphere is affected by our mouth.

Matthew 21:16 contains a truth that has helped me tremen-
dously.

And said unto him, Hearest thou what these say? And
Jesus saith unto them, Yea; have ye never read, Out of the
mouth of babes and sucklings thou hast perfected praise?

As I looked up each word in the Greek dictionary, I was able
to paraphrase this verse: "Out of the mouth of not speaking
young Christians, you have completed, made perfect, and prepared the praise of God." "Not speaking" and "young" are
descriptions used for a child or toddler. This reveals that God has
prepared praise to be used even by those believers who have not
mastered their authority of words. This doesn't mean that once
we gain control of our tongue and learn to operate faith by speaking that we no longer need praise. It means that even as newborn
babes in Christ we can bring destruction on our pressure by putting praise in our mouth. As we mature in the things of God,
praise will mature as well, and we will have even more reasons to
praise God.

Studying Matthew 21:16 more thoroughly, I was further
impressed by the Hebrew meaning. Jesus was quoting from
Psalm 8:2:

Out of the mouth of babes and sucklings hast thou
ordained strength because of thine enemies, that thou
mightest still the enemy and the avenger.

The Hebrew translation of this verse can be paraphrased,
"Out of the mouth of the young child or infant, you have set up
and laid for a foundation the force, boldness, and loud strength
because of the enemy to stop by exertion [wear him out], make
to fail, cause to cease the enemy." Therefore, praise is a foundation of strength from our spiritual youth. Praise wears the devil
out, makes him fail, and causes him to cease! Praising Jesus stops
the devil by exertion! He can't hold up under the pressure of

praise! When you praise God for His goodness and His mercy, speaking out loud about God's greatness and strength, the devil begins to say, "I can't stand the pressure!"

We are given an example of this in II Chronicles 20. King Jehoshaphat found himself in quite a fix. The Moabites, the Ammonites, and the Meunites had surrounded the tribe of Judah. The pressure was mounting, threatening to destroy him and his kingdom. What the enemy didn't realize was that "Judah" means "celebrate" or "praise." The enemy thought he could defeat praise.

King Jehoshaphat began to seek God for an answer to the dilemma. We don't see him falling apart or crying the blues saying, "Why's everybody always picking on me?" Jehoshaphat goes to the one with all of the answers, and what does he say? First, he begins to tell God about how great and mighty He is. He is praising Him! In II Chronicles 20:12 is the clincher: honesty.

O our God, wilt thou not judge them? for we have no might against this great company that cometh against us; neither know we what to do: but our eyes are upon thee.

Their eyes were on God—not the Moabites, the Ammonites, the Meunites or the "Pressurites." Then, God speaks His instructions.

And he said, Hearken ye, all Judah, and ye inhabitants of Jerusalem, and thou king Jehoshaphat, Thus saith the Lord unto you, Be not afraid nor dismayed by reason of this great multitude; for the battle is not yours, but God's. To morrow go ye down against them: behold, they come up by the cliff of Ziz; and ye shall find them at the end of the brook, before the wilderness of Jeruel. Ye shall not need to fight in this battle: set yourselves, stand ye still, and see the salvation of the Lord with you, O Judah and Jerusalem: fear not, nor be dismayed; to morrow go out against them: for the Lord will be with you. And Jehoshaphat bowed his head with his face to the ground: and all Judah and the inhabitants of Jerusalem fell before the Lord, worshipping the Lord. II Chronicles 20:15-18

Let's summarize God's instructions:

1. Don't be afraid;
2. Don't be dismayed (filled with dread, apprehension, or anxiety);
3. The battle is not yours (not your responsibility), but God's;
4. You shall not need to fight: Set yourselves.

The word "set" in verse 17 means "to station, place, offer, continue, remain." God was instructing him to remain in that position of praise—to continue to offer praise to God—and then he would see the salvation of the Lord.

So, what does Jehoshaphat do? He prepares the people of Judah in formation to march against the enemy. He doesn't send out the chariots or archers or men of war to the front; Jehoshaphat sends the singers and praisers out on the front lines of battle.

> *And when they began to sing and to praise, the Lord set ambushments against the children of Ammon, Moab, and mount Seir, which were come against Judah; and they were smitten. For the children of Ammon and Moab stood up against the inhabitants of mount Seir, utterly to slay and destroy them: and when they had made an end of the inhabitants of Seir, every one helped to destroy another. And when Judah came toward the watch tower in the wilderness, they looked unto the multitude, and, behold, they were dead bodies fallen to the earth, and none escaped.* II Chronicles 20:22-24

Did you notice that God didn't start moving until the praisers began praising? As they began to sing and praise, the enemy turned on each other until they were completely destroyed.

Remember what Psalm 8:2 says? Praise wears the enemy out by exertion and causes him to cease.

Jehoshaphat's story goes on to explain the benefits of overcoming pressure. As they searched the defeated enemy, they found a multitude of treasures that took three days to collect. The Bible says it was more than they could carry, and it all became theirs because they overcame the pressure in their lives.

There are many other examples of praise overcoming pressure: David overcame the pressure of Ziklag and recovered all that belonged to him; Joshua and the children of Israel overcame the pressure of Jericho by their shout of praise; the apostle Paul overcame persecution and imprisonment through his prayer and praise. You don't have to wait another day! You can lift your hands, let the praises ring, and watch your pressures scatter.

14 Prayer vs. Pressure

A handbook on anti-pressure strategies would be incomplete without disclosing God's secret weapon: prayer. While many people have been deceived by enemy propaganda that prayer is useless, repetitious, religious drudgery, God is equipping His armed forces with the tremendous, dynamic power available in this highly effective weaponry. Thankfully, the Holy Spirit is offering hands-on, one-on-one training in which He is personally overseeing your comfort and confidence in utilizing God's secret weapon with accuracy.

> *Confess your faults one to another, and pray one for another, that ye may be healed. The effectual fervent prayer of a righteous man availeth much.* James 5:16

The Amplified Bible says, "The earnest, [heartfelt, continued] prayer of a righteous man makes tremendous power available [dynamic in its working]." That tremendous power is available to help us overcome the pressures of life! The great thing is this: We are not on our own in prayer! Jesus sent us a Helper.

> *And in the same way—by our faith—the Holy Spirit helps us with our daily problems and in our praying. For we don't even know what we should pray for, nor how to pray as we should; but the Holy Spirit prays for us with such feeling that it cannot be expressed in words.* Romans 8:26 TLB

God is aware of the things you and I face on a daily basis. In fact, He is more aware of the events in our lives than we are because He sees things before they happen. God has never planned for us to be entangled with burdens and frustrations that sap our strength. Prayer is designed as a two-way communication through which we receive strength and direction for our lives.

Daniel was a man who understood the power unleashed in his communication with God. Something in his life was propelling him to excellence and honor. Under the reign of King Nebuchadnezzar, King Belshazzar, and King Darius, Daniel prospered and rose in rank over the entire country. Excuse me? Daniel was taken captive by Nebuchadnezzar. Yes, he was a slave, and they kept putting him in charge. You better believe Daniel faced his share of pressure. Do you think the other people on the king's staff were in agreement with a slave being put over them? That is what King Darius was preparing to do. Evidently Daniel's enemies began to suspect that prayer was Daniel's secret to success because that is what they attacked in his life.

When a nation prepares to engage in armed conflict with an opposing force, they evaluate the enemy's strongest points and target them for destruction. For instance, they will locate the airfields and destroy their ability to get planes into the air. They will locate fuel or ammunition storage centers and destroy those supplies. This cripples the strength of that opposing army. They are now limited in their ability.

Your enemy is using these same strategies against you. He has various forms of keeping us from our prayer time because he knows that prayer makes tremendous power available to us! Maybe you think prayer is boring or too hard or you have too many priorities to find time to pray. As a result, your life looks like that bombed out runway and you live off a one-day supply of spiritual rations for a week. Go ahead and say it: Ouch!

Daniel faced an intense pressure to not pray. He was facing death at the mouth of a hungry den of lions for talking to God. But Daniel made prayer the top priority in his life. He knew that without prayer he was without strength or power to overcome the pressure in his life. If you have struggled with your praying, you can rearrange your priorities right now. Prayer is your connection to overcoming pressure. Pray today!

Notice, though, that prayer wasn't the escape from facing pressure. Daniel kept praying and found himself at the edge of the lions' den. Sometimes we think God has failed us because we are facing a hard time: A lot of good prayer has done for me. Here I am getting ready to be thrown in this pit. However, prayer prepares us to defeat pressure, not escape pressure. Daniel's strength kept him calm and assured as he stepped into the pressure and said, "Pressure? No problem!" King Darius was worried all night, pacing the floor. Daniel wasn't worried. He was confident.

> *And this is the confidence that we have in him, that, if we ask any thing according to his will, he heareth us And if we know that he hear us, whatsoever we ask, we know that we have the petitions that we desired of him.* I John 5:14-15

Daniel's strong confidence was a result of time spent with God. This is the same confidence exemplified in the life of our Savior Jesus Christ. Jesus was dedicated to prayer, and we should conform to His image. Jesus tells us that prayer will help us to not enter into the temptations in our life.

> *Watch and pray, that ye enter not into temptation: the spirit indeed is willing, but the flesh is weak.* Matthew 26:41

> *Keep alert and pray. Otherwise temptation will overpower you. For the spirit indeed is willing, but how weak the body is!'* Matthew 26:41 TLB

Prayer will help us avoid being overtaken by the traps and snares of life. God can direct us and send instructions to us through prayer. Jesus, in this text, is facing the most intense pressure ever faced by a man. Jesus is facing the pressure of the cross, the pressure of death, the pressure of having the curse of sin, sickness, and disease laid on Him, and the pressure of being separated from the Father. Jesus dealt with His pressure through prayer.

Without prayer, you have no hope of overcoming the pressures in your life. Jesus went to the Father in prayer. We, too, must go to the Father in prayer. God wants to talk to you about your problems. He wants to be your advisor. He wants to be your assurance. He wants to be your confidence.

Jesus set such a strong standard for prayer that His disciples, who before had fallen asleep when Jesus asked them to pray, were later praying their way into victory over adversities. If you look at the kinds of struggles and pressures faced by the early Church, you know that the enemy desperately tried to stop their progress. They faced resistance on every side and yet prevailed in every dilemma.

Acts 12 holds an inspiring account of prayer prevailing over adversity. King Herod captured and imprisoned Peter. Having just executed James, the brother of John, Herod's plans for Peter were not pleasant. But God's plans for Peter prevailed over Herod's plans because tremendous power was made available.

Peter therefore was kept in prison: but prayer was made without ceasing of the church unto God for him. Acts 12:5

Peter was sleeping in the prison under heavy guard when an angel woke him up. The angel loosed his chains and opened every locked door as he led him out of the prison and to the gate of the city. Peter realized that he wasn't dreaming or having a vision when he was left standing in the street—free. But when Peter shows up at the house where all of his friends are praying, they don't believe it is him. Rhoda comes to the gate and gets so excited that Peter is actually standing there that she forgets to let him in. She leaves him standing there while she goes to tell everybody that their prayer has been answered. Picture those friends: "Rhoda, you are crazy! Now, leave us alone; we are praying for Peter!"

Do you really expect your prayer to change things? When the answer shows up do you figure, "That was too easy!" and go back to waiting on God? When Peter's friends finally came to the door, they were astonished. Hello! Wasn't that what you asked God for? It is like the surprise on a child's face as they push the buttons on the television for the first time and suddenly the set begins blaring as they run in the other direction. When you push that button, guess what! The power comes on! When you pray to God, guess what! Your prayers get answered.

And in that day ye shall ask me nothing. Verily, verily, I say unto you, Whatsoever ye shall ask the Father in my name, he will give it you. Hitherto have ye asked nothing in my name: ask, and ye shall receive, that your joy may be full. John 16:23-24

Power is available for you. Elijah tapped into this power and stopped the course of nature. Hannah received power to have Samuel and overcame the pressure of her barrenness. Samson prayed for God to strengthen him one last time, and he defeated more of the enemy in his death than in his entire life. All of these prayed under the old covenant. Now, we have a covenant established on better promises. We can boldly enter the throne room of God to get our help.

So let us come boldly to the very throne of God and stay there to receive his mercy and to find grace to help us in our times of need. Hebrews 4:16 TLB

Go in today and begin strengthening your relationship with your Heavenly Father. Overcoming the pressure of your life is no problem when you get God involved.

Jesus vs. Pressure 15

M any people have influenced the world we live in, but, none like our Lord Jesus Christ. Jesus, being the great leader that He is, established a pattern for the church to follow. As we model our lives, attitude, and beliefs after this pattern, we begin to operate in the victory He intends for our life.

Traditions have taught many people that Jesus could do this and that differently than you and I because He was so much more powerful than you and I are today. The Bible tells us something different. Jesus modeled for us how to live, love, and minister so that He could take His position as commander—head of the Church—and we could represent Him in victory here on earth. The Church is His Body. The authority and power given to Jesus is in you and I as believers. Jesus instructs us to be world changers!

> *In solemn truth I tell you, anyone believing in me shall do the same miracles I have done, and even greater ones, because I am going to be with the Father. You can ask him for anything, using my name, and I will do it, for this will bring praise to the Father because of what I, the Son, will do for you.* John 14:12 TLB

> *And he said unto them, Go ye into all the world, and preach the gospel to every creature. He that believeth and is baptized shall be saved; but he that believeth not shall be damned. And these signs shall follow them that believe; In my name shall they cast out devils; they shall speak*

with new tongues; They shall take up serpents; and if they drink any deadly thing, it shall not hurt them; they shall lay hands on the sick, and they shall recover. So then after the Lord had spoken unto them, he was received up into heaven, and sat on the right hand of God. And they went forth, and preached every where, the Lord working with them, and confirming the word with signs following. Amen. Mark 16:15-20

Jesus is preparing us. I believe this is why He birthed this book in my heart; to prepare His people to become world changers by overcoming pressure. If you can overcome pressure in your own life, you can use your faith and knowledge to help and train others to defeat pressures in their lives. Before I gave my heart to Jesus, my life was one disaster after another. At the age of twenty-three, I had been addicted to drugs for eight years, had witnessed the overdose death of my first husband, had lost custody of my children, and was facing three counts of attempted armed robbery. I came to God with more pressure than most people will ever face in their entire lives. I had attempted suicide three times. I overdosed on cocaine twice and was resuscitated by CPR. I had experienced guns against my temple and knives to my face.

Today, I co-pastor Faith Builders International, teach college classes at Faith Builders International Ministerial Academy, travel the U.S. preaching the gospel, direct inner city outreaches, as well as raise my children and love my husband. Do you know how I made it from there to here? Jesus showed me how to defeat pressure, adversity, and destruction by the Word of God.

While studying the Word, I discovered that Jesus fought battles and met with resistance just like I do. I found out that Jesus endured the opinions of others. Not everyone liked Him. Jesus had to put up with people just like you and I have to. An angry mob tried to throw Jesus off a cliff. The religious leaders were continuously trying to trick Him and get Him in trouble. Maybe that sounds like some people you have to put up with on your job.

Jesus also had the pressure of people depending on Him. Crowds came from miles away to hear Him preach, and they stayed even after they ran out of food. Jesus provided for the needs of these people.

Jesus never allowed outside pressure to get the best of Him. Neither did He allow the pressure of His flesh to get the best of Him. Some of the worst pressure we face is not from the devil; it is our flesh trying to run things. Jesus dealt with His flesh from the beginning. He fasted and prepared Himself to maintain control of His vessel.

That every one of you should know how to possess his vessel in sanctification and honour. I Thessalonians 4:4

Of all the lessons we can learn from the life of Jesus, one of the most freeing truths to grasp is that we can live in this flesh without succumbing to the pressures of our flesh. If we are supposed to know how to possess our "vessel," perhaps we should take a closer look at the Word of God for some instruction on how to resist the pressures of our flesh.

The term "possess" used in this verse has an interesting connotation. It is defined as "to get, to obtain, to acquire, to purchase, to provide." The term "vessel" means "equipment, implement, or apparatus." Let's see how this will affect the context of this instruction. The Word of God is indicating that each of us has a responsibility to get control of and obtain control of our equipment or tools that God has given us for this earth walk. In other words, it is not God's place to help us control our tempers, our emotions, or our desires. Thankfully, although it is not His responsibility, He helps us and provides the strength to do so through His Word.

Another definition used for "possess" is "to purchase." How does that apply to my flesh? Acquiring the reins of your flesh comes with a price. I realize that Jesus has paid for my salvation, and my gift of eternal life is covered by His sacrifice. I know that I have victory over my flesh through the life of Christ Jesus living in me. Still, it doesn't simply jump out of my Bible or out of my inner man and take over my flesh.

When I first became born again, I thought that everything could be solved if the preacher could lay hands on me. I took all of my problems to the prayer line. As a newborn Christian, God's mercy covered me many times. But I soon discovered that no one, no matter how anointed they were, could pray my flesh away. As I have grown in the things of God, I have learned that taking dominion begins by having my spirit take dominion of my flesh. If I can't exercise authority over sleeping late, poor eating habits, or lazy prayer time, then how capable will I be to have dominion over sickness and disease?

The works (products) of the flesh are described in Galatians 5:19-21.

> *Now the works of the flesh are manifest, which are these;*
> *Adultery, fornication, uncleanness, lasciviousness, Idolatry,*
> *witchcraft, hatred, variance, emulations, wrath, strife,*
> *seditions, heresies, Envyings, murders, drunkenness, revel-*
> *lings, and such like: of the which I tell you before, as I have*
> *also told you in time past, that they which do such things*
> *shall not inherit the kingdom of God.*

Let's zoom in on one in particular: "lasciviousness," which is best summed up as "no restraint." That is the direction your flesh will lead you if you yield to its desires. Romans 8 warns us that our flesh is an enemy to the direction of the Holy Spirit. When I was a child, the lack of restraint turned into rebellion. As a teenager that rebellion led me to run away from home. The more I yielded to the desires of my senses, the more those desires ruled me. This "no restraint syndrome" leads people into alcoholism, drug addiction, sexual perversions, murder, and so on.

Of course, I had no force in my life to produce resistance to that lasciviousness. Because of my parents' divorce, discipline was not a constant force. There was no Word in my life at that point. After I ran away from home, restraint was a thing of my past. By the time I received Jesus as my Lord, my senses were screaming "no restraint!" Addicted to drugs, both illegal and prescription, my life was a miserable mess. For the previous eight years my flesh had dictated my every waking moment. My flesh had determined how I spent my time, how I spent my money, and how the relationships in my life went. Like a freight train at full speed, my flesh had great momentum in my life. That freight train came to a screeching halt when I gave Jesus lordship of my life.

Here's the key: My flesh had been influenced by the devil for twenty-three years. Now the devil had lost his momentum. But, I had to yield my flesh to the lordship of Jesus on a daily basis in order to keep control of it. Then the momentum could build speed going in the other direction! That freight train doesn't start quickly, but when it gets going there is strength behind it. Every day, my spirit gained strength over my flesh. The Word became the dominant force over my senses.

Here's the good news. The price is not too expensive for any of us to pay. As a matter of fact, the two main ingredients are time and effort. To possess our vessel we must invest time in the Word of God and the effort of acting on His Word. God provides the power of His Word, and we invest our attention and obedience. There is no other way to gain dominion over your natural desires and senses than the Word way.

If you don't purposefully place your spirit in control of your soul—the mind, will and emotions—then your flesh will control your soul. So, ask yourself, "Who is in control?" Since the adversary can't get directly your spirit, he wants to find another way to destroy your life. If he can push the buttons of your senses, then he can gain access to your soul, you will make a decision that leads to destruction. Pressure is one of the main tools that he uses to push our buttons.

Whether the weakness of your flesh has been some form of addiction (overeating, gossip, and worry are included) or if, like the apostle Paul, you can't seem to do what you want to do and end up doing what you don't want to do, there is victory over the pressures of your flesh available for you in God's Word.

16 World Changers Conquer Pressure

Another world changer we can investigate is the apostle Paul. Who would have thought that God would have plans for this man who was running around putting Christians in jail? As a matter of fact, he was involved in the murder of Stephen. Today we would call him an accessory to murder.

But, after Jesus changed him, watch out! Paul became a world-changing machine. But look at the pressure that mounted when Paul started doing things for God. Suddenly the people who used to cheer him on were trying to kill him. His friends had to lower him over the city walls in a basket. People became so angry with him in one city that they stoned him until they thought he was dead. Believers gathered around him as he lay lifeless on the ground and prayed for him. Paul got up and went to the next city.

Paul became a professional at rising above the pressure. One day as Paul was preaching, a girl who was demon possessed began following him. A few days later, Paul cast the devil out of her. Isn't that what Mark 16 tells us to do? Instead of people being thankful, they got mad and threw Paul and Silas into prison after beating them with a whip. Paul didn't weep, complain, or grumble about his predicament. He didn't question God, either. Paul's reaction to the pressure of the moment was to pray and praise. I believe that Paul and Silas prayed for God to give them the victory and then began to rejoice that they received it. They were so loud that the other people in the prison heard them. They began to pressure their pressure with the spiritual forces in them. Suddenly the earth shook, the chains that bound them were broken, and all of the prisoners were set free.

As they overcame the pressure of their situation, those around them were affected by their victory. God wants that to happen in our lives as well. When we get freedom, our families get freedom. When we get freedom, our brothers and sisters in Christ get it, too.

Paul goes on to face riots at Thessalonica and Ephesus. He testifies to the church elders in Miletus saying:

And now, behold, I go bound in the spirit unto Jerusalem, not knowing the things that shall befall me there: Save that the Holy Ghost witnesseth in every city, saying that bonds and afflictions abide me. But none of these things move me, neither count I my life dear unto myself, so that I might finish my course with joy, and the ministry, which I have received of the Lord Jesus, to testify the gospel of the grace of God. And now, behold, I know that ye all, among whom I have gone preaching the kingdom of God, shall see my face no more. Acts 20:22-25

Paul knew the pressure that lay ahead and said, "None of these things move me." Nothing moved him away from his purpose. Paul goes on trial before Festus, Felix, and King Agrippa before being sent to stand trial in Rome. Paul resists the pressure of the storm that causes the ship he is sailing in to wreck. He stands on God's Word for the people on board to make it through the shipwreck alive. On the island where they found themselves shipwrecked, a poisonous snake sinks its teeth into Paul's arm. Paul just shakes it off. I guess after overcoming a storm and a shipwreck, the pressure of a snakebite was no problem.

Paul writes in Romans 8:37-39:

Nay, in all these things we are more than conquerors through him that loved us. For I am persuaded, that neither death, nor life, nor angels, nor principalities, nor powers, nor things present, nor things to come, Nor height, nor depth, nor any other creature, shall be able to separate us from the love of God, which is in Christ Jesus our Lord.

Paul also writes:

We are troubled on every side, yet not distressed; we are
perplexed, but not in despair; Persecuted, but not forsaken;
cast down, but not destroyed. II Corinthians 4:8-9

We truly are more than conquerors through Jesus. No matter what comes against us, we can prevail because the Greater One lives in us.

Paul writes these stirring words in II Timothy 4:7:

I have fought a good fight, I have finished my course, I
have kept the faith.

Paul resisted pressure and made it to his destiny—his destination. We can do ALL that Jesus has called us to do. We have the nature of the overcomer in us. We have been positioned with the victory that overcomes the world. That challenge is not our limit. It is only our stepping-stone. Let's start walking on the waters of our adversity and shake off the poison of our pressure. It is time to change the world with the Word!

A Pressure Preparation Checklist   17

Before pressure comes your way, be prepared. Here are a few things that will help you take inventory for pressure preparation. Of course, there are specific things in the life of every individual that the Holy Spirit will point out to help you be prepared. But this checklist is a good starting point.

1. Is your foundation stable?

Therefore whosoever heareth these sayings of mine, and doeth them, I will liken him unto a wise man, which built his house upon a rock: And the rain descended, and the floods came, and the winds blew, and beat upon that house; and it fell not: for it was founded upon a rock. And every one that heareth these sayings of mine, and doeth them not, shall be likened unto a foolish man, which built his house upon the sand: And the rain descended, and the floods came, and the winds blew, and beat upon that house; and it fell: and great was the fall of it. Matthew 7:24-27

Your foundation is the most important part of your life. Jesus teaches us that our foundation is based on hearing and doing His Word. Notice that in this example the pressure of the wind, the floods, and the rain were the same in both cases. In both instances the Word was heard, but it is the hearer who acts on the Word they have heard that strengthens their foundation against the pressures of the storm.

Storms are bound to come whether you are saved or not. But when the battle stops and the smoke clears, the hearer/doer will still be standing while the hearer is picking up the pieces of his life. That is a decision you and I must make for ourselves.

2. Are your contents explosive under pressure?

I like to explain this as the "sponge effect." What comes out of you when pressure is applied to your life? If the sponge is full of water, then water comes out. If the sponge is full of paint, then paint comes out. In that same way, if you are full of fear, then fear comes out. If you are full of bitterness, then bitterness comes oozing out.

The Bible tells us to be filled with the Holy Spirit.

And be not drunk with wine, wherein is excess; but be filled with the Spirit. Ephesians 5:18

In Acts 2:4 and 13:9, we see evidence of the early believers being filled with the Holy Spirit. If I am filled with the Holy Spirit, He is what will be released when pressure is applied to my life.

John 15:1-7 tells us that if we are full of the Word then we will produce fruit.

I am the true vine, and my Father is the husbandman. Every branch in me that beareth not fruit he taketh away: and every branch that beareth fruit, he purgeth it, that it may bring forth more fruit. Now ye are clean through the word which I have spoken unto you. Abide in me, and I in you. As the branch cannot bear fruit of itself, except it abide in the vine; no more can ye, except ye abide in me. I am the vine, ye are the branches: He that abideth in me, and I in him, the same bringeth forth much fruit: for without me ye can do nothing. If a man abide not in me, he is cast forth as a branch, and is withered; and men gather them, and cast them into the fire, and they are burned.If ye abide in me, and my words abide in you, ye shall ask what ye will, and it shall be done unto you.

The fruit produced by abiding in Jesus is listed in Galatians 5:16-23. This fruit provides stability in pressure.

> *But the fruit of the Spirit is love, joy, peace, longsuffering, gentleness, goodness, faith, Meekness, temperance: against such there is no law.* Galatians 5:22-23

Love

> *Love suffereth long, and is kind; love envieth not; love vaunteth not itself, is not puffed up, doth not behave itself unseemly, seeketh not its own, is not provoked, taketh not account of evil; rejoiceth not in unrighteousness, but rejoiceth with the truth; beareth all things, believeth all things, hopeth all things, endureth all things. Love never faileth: but whether there be prophecies, they shall be done away; whether there be tongues, they shall cease; whether there be knowledge, it shall be done away.* 1 Corinthians 13:4-8 ASV

Love is God. God is love. This is not the emotional experience that many call love. Love can withstand all pressure. Verse 7 says love bears all things. This love is a force produced in your spirit by the Word dwelling or abiding in you. This supernatural force never fails.

God's love has withstood every pressure since the beginning of time. It was God's love in His new covenant that brought a blood covering to the old covenant people. It was God's love that completed the plan of redemption through Jesus, with his out-pouring of blood that cleanses us from sin.

God's love isn't "out there" somewhere. God's love is in a place where pressure can't limit, hinder, or interrupt it. God has shed abroad His love in our hearts. "Shed" is defined as "poured out." God's supernatural force of love is poured out in our spirits.

So, how does this love of God enable us to overcome pressure and stress in our lives? When released through our lives, The love that God has for us causes us to respond to normal situations in a supernatural way. Jesus tells us to love our enemies and bless those who curse us (Luke 6:27-28). This requires love beyond that which our human nature possesses. How many would be honest and admit that there have been people and predicaments that have made us wonder, "How do you expect me to stay saved with this in my life?" Thank God for supernatural love beyond our limits.

Joy

> *Then he said unto them, Go your way, eat the fat, and*
> *drink the sweet, and send portions unto them for whom*
> *nothing is prepared: for this day is holy unto our Lord:*
> *neither be ye sorry; for the joy of the Lord is your strength.*
> Nehemiah 8:10

Joy is not happiness. The word "happiness" is derived for the root "hap" or "happen." Happiness is dependent on what happens in your life. Joy is a supernatural force that will cause you to rejoice despite what happens.

> *If you faint in the day of adversity, your strength is small.*
> Proverbs 24:10 NKJV

The joy of the Lord is our strength (Nehemiah 8:10). Joy gives us the stability in times of trouble. According to Proverbs 24:10, would this mean then that if you faint in the day of adversity or pressure your joy is small?

Joy is a force released because of God's Word and Spirit in our inner man. God gives us a method to keep our joy flowing: rejoicing. Get it? Re-joice. David displays a perfect example of this method. When everything important in his life was taken from him and all those who were his support system turned on him, David was faced with the perfect opportunity to cave in. But, in his desperation, David turned to the method that had seen him through so many other hopeless situations. David encouraged himself in the Lord. Rejoicing gave David the strength to pursue, overtake, and recover all.

Peace

And the peace of God, which surpasses all understanding,
will guard your hearts and minds through Christ Jesus.
Philippians 4:7 NKJV

Peace which surpassed all understanding is peace that you can't explain. The Amplified Bible says that the peace "shall garrison and mount guard" over your heart and mind. This is not simply an absence of trouble. In the midst of turmoil, your heart and mind will be guarded by this force of peace flowing from your spirit.

Jesus speaks of supernatural peace in John 16:33.

These things I have spoken unto you, that in me ye might
have peace. In the world ye shall have tribulation: but be
of good cheer; I have overcome the world.

Jesus has spoken and declared His Word to give us a peace that passes understanding in the midst of pressure. You and I can face the pressures of our daily lives and any dilemmas that arise because there is a force of peace that flows from our spiritual connection to the Lord Jesus. That means we have peace despite the pressure.

In John 14:27, Jesus explains, "Peace I leave with you, my peace I give unto you: not as the world giveth, give I unto you. Let not your heart be troubled, neither let it be afraid." The disciples who were gathered around Him understood a definition of this peace that you and I could benefit from knowing. This word "peace" implies being set at one in your health, welfare, and safety. In the Hebrew culture, this term was used as a written and verbal greeting much like today many would say "hello." The difference is that when people would greet each other with "peace," they were inquiring of that person, "Is it well with you? Do you have the peace that comes from being made whole?"

We see this supported throughout the Word of God. In Genesis 43:27, Joseph's brothers come to greet him. "And he

asked them of their *welfare*, and said, Is your father well, the old
man of whom you spake? Is he yet alive?" (emphasis added). The
word "welfare" is the Hebrew word that means "safety, prosperity,
well-being, intactness, and wholeness." In Exodus 18:7, "Moses
went out to meet his father-in-law and did obeisance, and kissed
him: and they asked each other of their *welfare*; and they came
into the tent" (emphasis added). So, we can see that when the
term "peace" is used, the picture they gained in their mind is that
"all is well, all is whole." One of my favorite preachers uses this
phrase, "Nothing missing, nothing broken!"

We discussed in an earlier chapter the focused faith of the
Shunammite woman from II Kings chapter 4. Let's look at her
response in the light of peace.

> *And she called unto her husband, and said, send me, I*
> *pray thee, one of the young men, and one of the asses,*
> *that I may run to the man of God, and come again. And*
> *he said, Wherefore wilt thou go to him to day? It is nei-*
> *ther new moon, nor Sabbath. And she said, [it shall be]*
> *well.* II Kings 4:22-23

In this verse, that actual translation of the phrase "it shall be"
uses one word that covered the complete meaning. This word is
the same word used in our previous references to peace, shalom!
This is the declaration of this woman, "I have the peace that
comes from being made whole. I refuse to be missing the life of
my son." When Gehazi is sent to confront her with the prophet's
inquiry, he comes to ask, "Is it well with you? Is it well with your
husband? Is it well with your son?" Translate and meditate. "Do
you have nothing missing? Does your husband have nothing broken? Does your son have the peace that comes from being made
whole?" This is covenant talk! Her response remains steadfast. "It
is well."

Now, let's take that understanding and apply it to the words
Jesus has given us. In John 14:27: Peace—all is well, all is whole in
your family, finances, health, your entire life—I have given unto

you. What Jesus has given us, no one can take away! We must become as convinced as the covenant woman and declare His peace in the midst of our pressure!

The truth you don't determine to know and understand is the truth the adversary can steal (see Matthew 13:19). You have to make up your mind to comprehend and receive this peace that comes from being made whole—despite what your circumstances say. Jesus said you already have His peace. Believe Him above the natural report!

Longsuffering = Patience

> *But let patience have her perfect work, that ye may be perfect and entire, wanting nothing.* James 1:4

I have met too many people who were taught not to pray for patience. They were told that if you pray for patience, God will put you through misery so you can learn patience. What a relief it is to those people when they learn that patience is produced by the Word living in your heart. Patience is a fruit of the spirit. We don't have to pray for it. We do have to put it to work in our lives. This verse says that patience will produce maturity. The word "perfect" here carries the meaning of completeness and maturity.

Have you noticed that a mature person can handle pressures of life more responsibly than an adolescent? We are all at various stages of development and levels of maturity. Don't feel condemned if another person is handling pressure better than you. Start working your patience and keep abiding in the vine. Patience will be developed in you.

The word "longsuffering," used here to describe the fruit or product of our born-again spirit, means "patience, forbearance, internal and external control in a difficult circumstance." We can easily perceive how valuable this force of patience is to a person who is facing pressure to quit, give in, or act out of desperation. The definition goes further to explain that "this control could exhibit itself by delaying an action."

I have experienced the greatest amounts of pressure when the adversary was trying to get me to move off of God's Word and react to what I could see, think, or feel. If he can't make me react to his pressure, then he can't get me off of God's path. What about that promise that doesn't come to pass the way you thought it would? Do you give up and walk away from believing? Longsuffering will hold your hand steady so that you stay the course.

Longsuffering is the power that makes the hard part easy. Waiting, enduring, persevering—who willingly chooses these options? Can you say to the Lord, "Oh, give me that promise that I must wait fifteen years for with no natural sign or indication that it really will happen other than your Word, Lord." To the natural part of us, there is nothing comfortable about waiting. Enduring paints a picture of Job on his ash heap, raking broken pottery over his boils. God has a different idea of endurance. Our heavenly Father has given us this spiritual substance of patience to supply us with the ease to endure, power to persevere, and willingness to wait. With this force of patience, I can outlast the devil. (He doesn't have any of this patience.) I can press forward longer than the devil can resist me. I can stand in faith longer than doubt can rage in my ears. I can hold on to God's Word as long as it takes!

Without this patience, how can we possess the promise? Hebrews 6:12 says, "That ye be not slothful, but followers of them who through faith and patience inherit the promises." You may have heard faith and patience described as "the power twins." Faith and longsuffering work together and enable us to acquire the covenant promises that rightfully belong to us. When you mix these two powerful forces together, you end up with confidence—a knowledge that is willing to wait, regardless of time, because it is sure that this promise will surely come to pass. It will happen! Time means nothing to a person who is filled with faith and patience. Only what God says counts!

Gentleness

Strong's Concordance gives us the definition of gentleness as follows:

Usefulness, moral excellence in character or demeanor, goodness, kindness

Many pressures we face are pressures to compromise our character. The force of gentleness produces the ability to stand against those pressures of compromise. Even as a gentleman maintains his morals and beliefs despite the situation, the fruit of gentleness helps us to remain useful under pressure.

Have you ever known anyone who was of no use when the going got tough? Paul encountered this with a young man named John Mark. Paul and Barnabas took John Mark with them on a missionary journey. When they encountered a little trouble in Pamphylia, he deserted them. Paul didn't want to be put in a position to depend on someone who would crumble under pressure.

And some days after Paul said unto Barnabas, Let us go again and visit our brethren in every city where we have preached the word of the Lord, and see how they do. And Barnabas determined to take with them John, whose surname was Mark. But Paul thought not good to take him with them, who departed from them from Pamphylia, and went not with them to the work. And the contention was so sharp between them, that they departed asunder one from the other: and so Barnabas took Mark, and sailed unto Cyprus; And Paul chose Silas, and departed, being recommended by the brethren unto the grace of God. And he went through Syria and Cilicia, confirming the churches. Acts 15:36-41

In Chapter 16 we talked about a demon-possessed girl following Paul. Think about what awaited Paul and Silas in Philippi when he cast the devil out of the girl. They were sent to prison. But they praised God and an earthquake set them free. What would have happened if John Mark had been with them and caved under the pressure? Paul and Silas were both praising God and releasing their faith when that earthquake happened. They were in agreement according to Matthew 18:18.

God wants to produce that stalwart strength in you so that you can be useful in your church, useful in your home, useful to pray for the sick, useful to raise the dead!

"Moral excellence" is another term used to define gentleness. I am sure that each of us could admit that when we came to Jesus there were areas of our moral character that were lacking in excellence. Maybe you had a hard time keeping your word, promising things you didn't fulfill. Perhaps you were the one that the town gossip cornered to trash talk all your church friends and you just sat there. Well, God's Spirit will produce moral excellence in our hearts when we allow Him to work on those areas. As you grow in the Lord, you will feel the Holy Spirit direct you to hold your tongue and not commit to certain appointments or responsibilities until you know for certain you can keep that commitment. You will feel the nudging of His spirit to kindly tell that town gossip, "I prefer to change the subject. If you would like to discuss something other than your opinion of other people, I would be glad to carry on a conversation. But I am not going to be a part of your gossip."

Perhaps it would benefit us to consider gentleness in this manner. Gentleness is the supernatural force to behave and respond to my fellow man in the way God would behave and respond in my situation. God will always respond justly and excellently, behaving Himself and controlling His emotions by His Word. When we allow His gentleness to work through us, we can disagree, explain our opinion, or stand for the Word way in a calm, gentle manner.

Goodness = Virtue

Strong's Concordance tells us that goodness means "virtue or beneficence." Well, I don't use either of those words on a regular basis. So, I looked them up in Webster's Illustrated Encyclopedic Dictionary.

Virtue = The quality of moral excellence, righteousness, responsibility, goodness

Beneficence = The quality of charity or kindness

While this sounds similar to gentleness, there is a difference. In the description of the virtuous woman of Proverbs 31, we see this characteristic very vividly.

Who can find a virtuous woman? for her price is far above rubies. The heart of her husband doth safely trust in her, so that he shall have no need of spoil. She will do him good and not evil all the days of her life. She seeketh wool, and flax, and worketh willingly with her hands. She is like the merchants' ships; she bringeth her food from afar. She riseth also while it is yet night, and giveth meat to her household, and a portion to her maidens. She considereth a field, and buyeth it: with the fruit of her hands she planteth a vineyard. She girdeth her loins with strength, and strengtheneth her arms. She perceiveth that her merchandise is good: her candle goeth not out by night. She layeth her hands to the spindle, and her hands hold the distaff. She stretcheth out her hand to the poor; yea, she reacheth forth her hands to the needy. She is not afraid of the snow for her household: for all her household are clothed with scarlet. She maketh herself coverings of tapestry; her clothing is silk and purple. Her husband is known in the gates, when he sitteth among the elders of the land. She maketh fine linen, and selleth it; and delivereth girdles unto the merchant. Strength and honour are her clothing; and she shall rejoice in time to come. She openeth her mouth with wisdom; and in her tongue is the law of kindness. She looketh well to the ways of her household, and eateth not the bread of idleness. Her children arise up, and call her blessed; her husband also, and he praiseth her. Many daughters have done virtuously, but thou excellest

> *them all. Favour is deceitful, and beauty is vain: but a*
> *woman that feareth the Lord, she shall be praised. Give*
> *her of the fruit of her hands; and let her own works praise*
> *her in the gates.* Proverbs 31:10-31

Goodness is not a force limited to a woman. Jesus operated in goodness all the time. Goodness compels us to help others and be kind to others. Acts 10:38 declares that "Jesus went about doing good and healing all that were oppressed by the devil".

One of our heavenly Father's main attributes is goodness. When Moses makes his request in Exodus 33 to see God's glory, God responds with a revelation of His goodness. Even as God declares His name in that moment, it is a display of His goodness. The Lord is good!

In a society bogged down with pressures of "have it your way today" and "just do it," we need a force that is compelling us to recognize the needs of others. Otherwise pressure would cause us to turn all our attention on ourselves. By allowing God's force of goodness to compel and direct our decisions, we prevent the sabotage of tension and pressure that arises from self-centered decisions and motivations.

Do we need some practical illustrations? In a society where the evening news reeks of one horror story after another, we have in-your-face examples of the destruction that comes in lives lacking this force of goodness: A teenager in Missouri smashes her newborn baby against the curb because she doesn't want the responsibility; A college student kills her newborn baby when she throws her in the dumpster; Foster parents were convicted of murder after duct taping a child's hands, feet and mouth before bed, and the child choked on his vomit in the middle of the night. Granted, these instances are extreme, but, do you get my point?

In the life of a believer, there must be this flow of God's nature marking us as distinct from the world. If any one should be prompt to do good, it should be the believer. Pressure will always steer you toward the selfish way. Beware! It's a trap! Always take the way where God's goodness can flow through you into the lives of others.

Faith

We've already discussed the workings of this force against pressure in great detail. Faith is the victory that overcomes!

> *And being not weak in faith, he [Abraham] considered not his own body now dead, when he was about an hundred years old, neither yet the deadness of Sarah's womb: He staggered not at the promise of God through unbelief; but was strong in faith, giving glory to God. And being fully persuaded that, what he had promised, he was able also to perform.* Romans 4:19-20

Fully persuaded, Abraham staggered not. How did he do that? What if we untied the "nots" in this scripture? The outcome would be much different: "And being weak in faith, he considered his own body now dead, when he was about an hundred years old, and the deadness of Sarah's womb: He staggered at the promise of God through unbelief." This gives us an insight into being fully persuaded.

God provides faith as a force flowing from our inner man. Nothing that exists can hinder that force as long as it is flowing. Your inner man is off limits to the enemy. Circumstances and situations will make every attempt to stop your faith. But when you know that your faith will prevail over every force that presses against your progress, you will keep going and going and going. So be strong in faith, not considering the strength of your situation. Don't stagger through unbelief, but take sure, accurate steps of faith. Progress is inevitable when you take God at His Word.

Meekness

Meekness is defined as humility. In I Peter 5:5 we find the importance of this fruit.

> *Likewise, ye younger, submit yourselves unto the elder. Yea,*
> *all of you be subject one to another, and be clothed with*
> *humility: for God resisteth the proud, and giveth grace to*
> *the humble.* I Peter 5:5

In my mind, I used to picture meekness as a pitiful, forlorn, use-me-like-a-doormat-and-I'll-just-live-with-it kind of attitude. Thankfully, that is not God's idea of being meek.

I have found that meekness is a necessary characteristic for spiritual growth. Meekness means being teachable; it is a willingness to be obedient, willingly coming under authority and being humbly submissive. In Numbers 12:3, we find that Moses was more meek than any other man. I would say that aided him immensely in pastoring three million people. Psalms 25:9 tells us that God can guide the meek.

> *But the meek shall inherit the earth: and shall delight*
> *themselves in the abundance of peace.* Psalm 37:11

When we cultivate the force that enables us to willingly come under God's authority, God can guide us into this abundance of peace. If we don't, then we position ourselves to struggle. God's plan for our lives is that we delight ourselves in His abundance of peace.

> *The Lord lifteth up the meek.* Psalms 147:6

When we have this willingness to be obedient and teachable, God can lift us up. When my children come tearing into the room in hopes that I can settle their disputes, I first have to hear their evidence. If I find that one has broken the rule and the other has done what I expected, I can lift up the one who obeyed me. God can defend us and pick us up much easier when we follow His Word.

I Peter 3:4 reveals that a meek spirit is "in the sight of God of great price." In fact, Ephesians explains that it is a necessary ingredient to walk worthy of our calling.

I therefore, the prisoner of the Lord, beseech you that ye walk worthy of the vocation wherewith ye are called, With all lowliness and meekness, with longsuffering, forbearing one another in love. Ephesians 4:1-2

The Holy Spirit admonishes us in I Timothy 6:11 to "follow after...meekness." To properly receive the Word so that it becomes "the engrafted Word" requires the force of meekness as James 1:21 indicates to us:

Wherefore lay apart all filthiness and superfluity of naughtiness, and receive with meekness the engrafted word, which is able to save your souls. James 1:21

Humility positions us for success in pressure. If we humble ourselves, God will exalt us. If we don't humble ourselves, pride will make us fall (see Proverbs 16:18). God doesn't make us fall. Our choice to remain unteachable will provide destruction. On the same hand, our choice to let the fruit of meekness grow will benefit us with God's promotion.

Temperance

I am so glad that God made this a fruit produced by the Word in our spirit. Temperance means self-control or self-discipline. We need to develop this in our lives at all times, but especially when pressure is being applied to our lives. Control those thoughts. Control that mouth. Control that anger. Control that eating. Control! Control! Control! We need some control!

Look at what we can expect if we don't have control:

A man without self-control is as defenseless as a city with broken-down walls. Proverbs 25:28 TLB

A city that has no walls is left defenseless against intruders and thieves. The verse says "defenseless." Isn't that what it feels like after you've lost your temper? Don't you feel defenseless after you have indulged in gossip? It's a lack of control.

As I spent more time abiding in the Word of God, I had more control over my thoughts, my emotions, and my behavior. Self-control is a must in a pressure situation.

3. Who is making the final decision?
Your spirit or your soul?

Check this out! Your spirit is designed by God to be the final decision-maker of your life! We are spirit, soul, and body.

> *And the very God of peace sanctify you wholly; and I pray God your whole spirit and soul and body be pre-served blameless unto the coming of our Lord Jesus Christ.* I Thessalonians 5:23

Your soul is not equipped to make right choices on its own. (Remember, your soul consists of your mind, will, and emotions.) The carnal mind without God's influence is an enemy against God.

> *For they that are after the flesh do mind the things of the flesh; but they that are after the Spirit the things of the Spirit. For to be carnally minded is death; but to be spiritually minded is life and peace. Because the carnal mind is enmity against God: for it is not subject to the law of God, neither indeed can be.* Romans 8:5-7

Your spirit must be trained by the instructions of God's Word to make the right choices for your life. Remember Eve and her decision. Get your spirit in the place of authority over your soul and body.

Finally, let me remind you. We are never instructed to be complacent in pressure. Ephesians 6:10-11 tells us to be strong and stand against the pressure of the enemy.

Finally, my brethren, be strong in the Lord, and in the power of his might. Put on the whole armour of God, that ye may be able to stand against the wiles of the devil.

James 4:7 instructs us to resist the devil. Resist his pressure and that pressure will have to leave. As long as you continue to allow pressure to build it will continue to grow and grow until you can't hold it anymore. Don't wait another day. Don't be like Pharoah. When asked by Moses when he wanted the plague of frogs to be done away with, Pharoah decided that tomorrow would be a good time (see Exodus 8). Why spend another night with the nasty frogs crawling around your house, in your bath tub, and in the kitchen sink? Get rid of this plague right now!

II Timothy 2:3 tells us to endure hardness as a good soldier. Soldiers fight for their cause. Be willing to fight for your future. Fight for your family, and fight with faith.

Your marriage is worth fighting for. Your health is worth fighting for. Your peace is worth fighting for. Pressure is an enemy you can whip through the power of the Word of God. Make up your mind today to declare:

"Pressure? No problem!"

Pressure? No Problem!
Order Form

Postal orders: Faith Builders Int'l.
P.O. Box 452
Desoto, KS 66018

Telephone orders: (913) 583-1670

E-mail orders: order@michellesteeleministries.com

Please send *Pressure? No Problem!* to:

Name: _____

Address: _____

City: _____ State: _____

Zip: _____ Telephone: (_____) _____

Book Price: $12.00

Shipping: $3.00 for the first book and $1.00 for each additional book to cover shipping and handling within US, Canada, and Mexico. International orders add $6.00 for the first book and $2.00 for each additional book.

Or order from:
ACW Press
1200 Hwy 231 South #273
Ozark, AL 36360

(800) 931-BOOK

or contact your local bookstore